To a

XXX

ABOUT THE AUTHORS

 Hendrika was born in Pretoria (South Africa) and spent her formative years in the North West Province where she earned her BA (HONS) degree in Social Sciences. She then received several qualifications in Education, TEFOL, Coaching and Adult Training. Hendrika and her young family left South Africa in 2006 for the lights of Paris, followed by the lure of England for a few more years. In 2009, the family relocated across the globe and settled in Melbourne, Australia.

She is a professional Master Certified Coach, who understands the daily struggles of non-English speakers, the effects of culture shock and migratory grief and loss on individuals and their families. She hopes to use this book as a starting tool to prepare migrants for the emotional rollercoaster of an international move, and for you to know, that you are not alone. Hendrika lives with her husband, daughter and two very spoilt cats, Max and Lucy.

Website: www.pillarsofpower.com.au

Robyn never spent two Christmases in the same house for the first 15 years of her married life. From humble beginnings in Durban (South Africa), Robyn has lived and worked in nine cities around the world, including London, Paris and Singapore.

Using her vast life experience, Robyn started Personnel Relocations in Melbourne in 2008, helping countless other families to move and settle.

Sharing her knowledge and expertise with families in this book, Robyn hopes never to hear the words: "Ah, I wish I knew you when I moved to Australia". Robyn lives SE of Melbourne with her husband, two teenagers and her best furry friend, Joy a Beagle.

Website: www.personnelrelocations.com.au

YOUR D.I.Y. MOVE
GUIDE TO AUSTRALIA

Robyn Vogels
and
Hendrika Jooste

Your D.I.Y. Move Guide to Australia

First published in Australia 2020 by:
Your Move Guide
PO Box 673, Ringwood
VIC 3134

Email: yourmoveguide@gmail.com
Website: www.yourmoveguide.com
Facebook: www.facebook.com/yourmoveguide/

ISBN: 9798670117913

Cover design by Sean Creighton
Illustrations by Kobus Galloway
Editing by Hendrika Jooste

Disclaimer:
Whilst every effort has been made to ensure the information contained in this book is accurate, and up to date, please note that the information contained here is intended only as general guidance. Laws, rules, policies and other information are subject to change and variation. Therefore, it is crucial that you carry out your own checks and due diligence in line with your circumstances at the time you take action. No liability or responsibility will be taken for any errors or loss, financial or otherwise, as a result of actions you have taken as a result of reading this book.

DEDICATION

We dedicate this book to our supportive families, both in Australia and South Africa, who have been on this journey with us. We thank you.

And to our fellow migrant family, friends, acquaintances and colleagues who have shared their stories to pay it forward to future migrants coming to Australia.

We would like to acknowledge the First Australians, the Aboriginal nation, as the traditional custodians of the continent, whose cultures are among the oldest living cultures in human history. We pay respect to the Elders of this nation and extend our recognition to their descendants.

WHAT OTHER READERS HAVE SAID

"I only have one regret, and that is that I did not find this book when we started our whole immigration process. I would have had a lot less sleepless nights and a lot more peace of mind."

"I can highly recommend that anyone is considering or starting the process of emigrating to Australia to read this book. The information it contains is so detailed and in my personal opinion, invaluable. I can only thank the authors for taking the time to write this great book."

"A great purchase! Takes the guessing work away and calmed my nerves considerably. Very useful info. Thank you!"

"Glad we bought this when we started. Very informative and easy to read. A real gem!"

"This is a great source of information for anyone thinking of or in the process of moving to Australia. I think the process of immigration is underestimated, and this helps you prepare as well as tell you where to find help when needed."

"My congratulations on a well-researched, informative and very practical guide! I think the book will have a tremendous influence on people's success, well-being and family relationships."

"Information received was priceless!"

CONTENTS

1

WELCOME TO AUSTRALIA

Dear Reader,

Congratulations! You have decided to embark on one of the most important journeys of your life, namely, to emigrate to Australia.

You have also made the best decision to purchase our book – thank you! Not only will this book be your guide, but it will also provide you with professional knowledge, practical hints and valuable information. It will help you to avoid unnecessary and costly mistakes.

We cringe when we see the open-ended questions and (mostly) outdated and uninformed replies given to prospective migrants on social media forums.

Between the two of us, as the authors, we have a total of 35 years of experience with international relocations. We have both experienced our own moves with children and pets across four continents, and we have helped and supported others with their relocations to Australia for over a decade.

This book is filled with practical advice on moving with children, expert tips and advice for the whole family and lots of funny migrant moments.

In short, we have made or seen most of the blunders, and we are here to share them with you, for your benefit, so you can avoid making the same mistakes. A smooth migration process equals less stress and more positive experiences for the whole family.

We encourage you to use this book as a guide. It does not offer set checklists or legal migration advice but will help you navigate your migration journey and take the guesswork out of your move.

We do provide some generic lists and timelines, but we are not at all prescriptive. At the end of each chapter, we give recommendations that we have found to be best practice, and which will prove to be the most useful or most productive on your journey.

At the time of publishing, the information provided in this guide was correct. We will update any changes in future editions.

YOUR MOVE GUIDE HISTORY

You might be surprised to know this is not our first book. It might also surprise you to know that our first book had a somewhat original title: "Moving your SH!T to Australia."

Our first book was aimed at South African migrants. In Africa, as in all other parts of the world, there is a beetle called the Dung Beetle. These little critters are strong, but sometimes they move more dung (poo) than they need. Bringing too much stuff on your migration journey wastes your money!

The dung beetle concept also extends to emotional issues, unresolved trauma, political views and rigid stereotyping. All these will hinder migrants from thoroughly enjoying their migration journey. In short, all the "unnecessary" stuff that should be left behind.

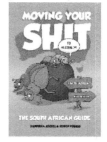

LET'S GET THE TERMINOLOGY RIGHT

Throughout this book, we will be using terminology that is common to settled migrants but could still be unknown to you.

According to the Merriam-Webster dictionary, the words "migrate", "emigrate" and "immigrate" are all about being on the move. All these terms originate from the Latin word "migrare", which means "to move from one place to another".

"Emigrate" and "immigrate" sound alike. Both words involve leaving one location and entering another.

The subtle difference between them lies in the point of view: "emigrate" stresses leaving the original place, while "immigrate" focuses on entering the new one.

An easy way to remember the difference is by means of the prefix e-, which means "away", as in "eject", and the prefix im-, which means "into" as in "inject".

The term "migrate" mostly refers to seasonal moving between jobs, seasons or places. In this book, we use "migrants" as a collective noun to describe all migrants who have moved to and settled in Australia.

There are **four types of migrants** in the world:

1. **Voluntary migrants** are those people who leave their country of origin (home or native country) to find employment, economic opportunities, or advanced education in another country. They are also the people who move to another country after marriage or to reunite with family members who have already emigrated, such as South Africans who permanently migrate to Australia.

2. **Refugees** are those who have been involuntarily displaced by persecution, war, or natural disasters, for example, the European migrants after World War II.

3. **Asylum seekers** are those who willingly leave their native country to flee persecution or violence, like the Sudanese and Myanmar migrants.

4. **Sojourners or ex-pats** are those who relocate to a new

country for a limited time and a specific purpose. It is important to note that this group fully intend to return to their home country.

WHAT ARE YOUR REASONS FOR CHOOSING AUSTRALIA?

You may have several reasons for choosing Australia in favour of the United Kingdom, Canada or New Zealand or anywhere else for that matter. On the other hand, you may also have only one goal, such as to join settled family members in Australia or for an employment opportunity.

Maybe you don't want to endure the long winters and knee-deep snow in Canada. Or you want sunny days instead of the grey skies of the United Kingdom and Europe. You probably can't imagine driving on the right side of the road like they do in the USA and Canada. You may worry that New Zealand is too far south and you don't want to endure the cold winters.

We hear it so many times: "Australia is great, and that is why we are moving to Australia." There is a lot of truth in that, but there is also still a lot to learn.

After your arrival, some Australians might ask why you chose Australia. When prompted, migrants will typically reply: "The weather, the educational system, clean environment and beaches, Australians also drive on the left side of the road, and the food is more or less the same."

However, the longer you live in Australia, the shorter your answer will become. When you first step off the aeroplane, you will arrive with preconceived ideas, stereotypes, assumptions, anticipated notions and even a few urban myths about your new life in Australia. Most migrants believe that Australia is the "promised" land, and with that mindset, they create many false expectations of Australia.

BACK TO YOUR FUTURE

Migration is equivalent to climbing into a modified DeLorean car with Marty McFly and Doc Brown from the movie *Back to the Future*, travelling back in time to an unknown destination.

However, your time machine will not work as well as in the movie. While Marty was a younger version of himself, you, on the other hand, will still be the same age. Depending on your age, you will step at least 15-20 years back in time regarding employment, finances (credit record), housing, social status and friendships.

However, you will realign your needs with this fresh start, so it's not all bad news! It also won't take you another 20 years to regain all you had in your home or native country.

Don't despair; you are not alone. It is a normal process and happens to all migrants who leave their native or home country. The process is different for every ethnic group, and the degree in which it affects individuals differs significantly. This phenomenon is called "culture shock". We discuss this further in Chapter 8.

REMIND YOURSELF OF THE SH!T

Remember how we said our first moving guide's title was: Moving your SH!T? How can you make it easier for yourself and your family? We have identified the following four essential things you have to keep in mind to make this important chapter in your lives as stress-free and as memorable as possible:

Sometimes it sucks

It sucks to be away from your family and friends and to feel alone and isolated. It sucks to speak English all day and every day when English is your Second (ESL) or even Third Language.

But it is also okay to sometimes feel that life as a migrant suck. We all have those days and moments. The critical thing to remember is to feel the emotion and to deal with it. Get up every day and try again. Don't hang on to the "sucky" feelings.

Humbleness and humour are virtues

Too many migrants arrive with egos as big as the Sydney

Opera House. Please leave your ego at the airport. It is not going to assist you or your family in any possible way.

Australians will welcome you with open arms, but if you try to enforce your values and opinions on them, they will not bend to your way of doing things.

The dictionary describes "humble" as "being not proud or haughty", "not arrogant or assertive". Patti McCarthy uses the terms "bend" or "snap" in her book *Cultural Chemistry*. If you don't bend, you are going to snap. It relates to your ability to change or be changed easily. Depending on the situation, your ability to be "flexible" will ensure if you bend or snap.

A synonym for "humble" is "meek". Remember, meekness is not a sign of weakness. To compromise is not about giving up or giving in but finding a different path. Find a different approach, with a huge dose of daily humour, and your life will be filled with "no worries, mate".

Identity is important

On your arrival in Australia, your identity is still going to be 100% of your native culture. Your identity is what makes you different, but also unique. Don't lose your identity in Australia. Speak your native language at home, attend religious, spiritual, and cultural activities, and invite new friends for dinner.

Seek music and entertainment events that are provided by entertainers from your home country who are touring Australia. A tree can't be replanted without its roots. The same goes for human beings. Within a family unit, we all have different personalities and needs. Every family member is an individual who has his or her own needs, goals, rights and responsibilities. We are all different.

Time, tenacity, and tact

One of the most revolutionary concepts that we learned in the 20th century is that time is not a universal measurement. It doesn't matter how much our lives are governed by the same seconds, minutes, hours, days, and weeks, regardless of where we live on the globe, time will never be absolute. The rate at which time passes depends entirely on your speed and acceleration at any given moment.

Give yourself time to adjust to new things, time to meet new people and time to adapt to a new culture. As long as you are tenaciously moving forward, it is okay.

The speed with which you are moving doesn't matter; it is how you go about it that counts. Pack some tact, and it will serve you well on this journey.

READY, SET, GO!

You've decided to move and to settle in Australia. You went through the administrative red tape and jumped through the hoops and conquered many hurdles to get your visa. You said your good-byes, you packed up your stuff and now you are sitting on the aeroplane to fly to Australia.

Are you ready for this rollercoaster migration ride?

Source:
Moving your SH!t to Australia: The South African Guide

If not, buckle up buttercup, because it is going to be a very bumpy ride. However, don't despair. You have this guide, and you can catch up with us on social media. So many, who came to Australia before you, did not prepare themselves as well as you did. You may never know the stress you will be missing out on – you are the lucky ones.

WE ARE HERE FOR YOU!

You have bought the book, so you automatically qualify to have access to the YOUR MOVE GUIDE VIP CHAT ROOM. This dedicated space is FREE to our readers. It is a place to connect with the authors and the panel of experts for all of your relocation questions.

We have FREE resources, GIVE-AWAYS and EVENTS throughout the year. Connect with us to find out how we can assist and support you and connect with others on the same journey to Australia and even meet up with them when you arrive!

How do you get in?
1. Using the Contact Us-page on our website:
   www.yourmoveguide.com/contact-us
2. Complete the necessary information and in the subject line type the **code** that you will find at the back of the book.

This book is only the first step. Reach out and connect. It is a conversation that costs nothing.

Welcome to the "lucky country"!

Hendrika and Robyn

2

AUSTRALIA: A CONTINENT

*"Australia, to the rest of the world, is just far away,
and Australia in the Thirties was the faraway of the faraway."*

~ Baz Luhrmann (Australian director & screenwriter)

To gain a deeper understanding of Australia and its diverse cultures, it is essential to relate to the history and understand some necessary background information.

Some might think that this is unimportant and irrelevant. However, if you have a deeper understanding of the inner workings of Australia, you will appreciate and value your new host country much more.

A BRIEF OVERVIEW OF AUSTRALIA
Australia is both the largest island and the smallest continent in the world, with a multi-cultural population of 22 million. The nearest neighbours are the South East Asian and Pacific nations, the closest of which are Indonesia, Papua New Guinea and New Zealand.

The Australian economy enjoys a clear competitive advantage in producing and processing primary products, due to an abundance of natural resources, together with a world-class transport and telecommunications infrastructure.

Australia is a federation represented by the federal government, with specific powers derived from a constitution, six states, two territory governments and local governments, with powers vested by the state and territory governments.

The country is one of the world's largest exporters of wool and meat, and a primary international source of gold, wheat, iron ore, bauxite, mineral sands, coal, alumina, rice, sugar and cotton.

Substantial export earnings are also derived from crude oil, paper products, plastics, chemical products, wine, services, tourism, and numerous forms of technology, biotechnology, manufactured items and computer software.

Major imports are motor vehicles, aircraft, manufacturing equipment and computer hardware.

A BRIEF HISTORY OF AUSTRALIA

Australia's Aboriginal people, believed to have arrived 50 000 years ago, have the oldest continuous culture on earth. When discovered by the British, there was a population of around one million, speaking 700 languages across 500 clans.

In 1770, Captain James Cook set foot on the island and claimed it as a British colony. On 26 January 1788, the new outpost was declared a penal colony and the first fleet of eleven ships arrived, carrying 1 500 people – half of which were convicts.

Over the next 60 years, more than 160 000 convicts were brought to Australia from all over Europe, resulting in a truly diverse culture still present today. The discovery of gold in 1851 also brought boatloads of Asians to Australia. What a truly worldly place to be in, with European convicts and Asian gold miners!

On the first of January 1901, the six states (provinces) and two territories became one nation under a single constitution.

Today, people from over 200 countries make up the Australian community, with more than 300 languages spoken across the country.

THE STATES AND TERRITORIES OF AUSTRALIA
Australia comprises of six states and two territories:

The Australian Capital Territory (ACT) is situated between Sydney and Melbourne. It is the site of the nation's capital city, Canberra. Canberra is home to important national institutions, such as Parliament House, the High Court of Australia, the Australian War Memorial and the National Gallery of Australia.

New South Wales (NSW) was the first colony to be established by the British under the control of a Governor. It is Australia's oldest and most populous state. Sydney is the capital city of New South Wales and is also the nation's largest city. The Sydney Harbour Bridge and Opera House are national icons.

The Northern Territory (NT) has the tropics in the north and red desert soil in the south. Most of its small population lives in the capital city, Darwin, and along the main highway between Darwin and Alice Springs, which is the main town near the centre of Australia.

Queensland (QLD) is the second-largest state (in size). It has the Torres Strait Islands in the north, extensive tropical rainforests, temperate coastal areas and an often dry inland. The world-famous Great Barrier Reef runs along its eastern coast, including the World Heritage-listed Fraser Island. The capital city is Brisbane.

South Australia (SA) has a rugged coastline and many famous wine regions. Adelaide, the capital city, has many examples of fine colonial architecture. From Adelaide, you can explore the Barossa wineries, The Flinders Ranges, and Kangaroo Island. South Australia is known as the "Festival State", with more than 500 events and festivals taking place every year.

Tasmania (TAS) is the smallest state, separated from the mainland by the Bass Strait. Much of the island has unspoilt wilderness landscapes. Tasmania's capital city is Hobart, and it is the smallest state in Australia.

Victoria (VIC) is the smallest of the mainland states, but it is home to the country's second most populated city, Melbourne. Many fine buildings in Victoria were built from the wealth created by the gold rush of the 1850s. Victoria's capital city is Melbourne and is often referred to as the nation's cultural capital.

Western Australia (WA) is the largest state and is a place of real contrasts. The eastern side is mostly desert, while the south-west is a rich agricultural and wine-producing area. The state is home to many large mining projects. About three-quarters of the state's population lives in Perth, the capital city. Off the coast of Esperance, is Middle Island, which is home to the pink-coloured Lake Hiller.

THE NATIONAL SYMBOLS OF AUSTRALIA

Flags
Australia has three official flags: the Australian National Flag, the Australian Aboriginal Flag and the Torres Strait Islander Flag. Each state and territory also has its own flag.

The Australian National Flag:
The flag is blue, white, and red. It has three important parts:

- The flag of Great Britain, known as the Union Jack, is in the top left corner. The flag represents the history of British settlement.
- The Commonwealth Star is below the Union Jack. This star has seven points, one point for each of the six states and one for the territories.
- The Southern Cross, on the right, is a group of stars that can be seen in the southern sky.

The Australian Aboriginal Flag:
This flag is black, red, and yellow. It has three important parts, and the most common interpretation of the colours is:

- The top half is black and represents the Aboriginal people of Australia.
- The bottom half is red and represents the earth and a spiritual relation to the land.
- The yellow circle represents the sun.

The Torres Strait Islander Flag:
The Torres Strait Islander Flag is green, blue, black, and white:

- The green stripes represent the land.
- The blue panel in the centre represents the sea.

- The black lines represent the Torres Strait Islander people.
- The white dancer's headdress in the centre is a symbol for all Torres Strait Islanders.
- The points of the white star represent the island groups in the Torres Strait.
- The colour white is a symbol of peace.

Commonwealth Coat of Arms

The Commonwealth Coat of Arms is the official symbol of the Commonwealth of Australia. It represents national unity and identifies the authority and property of the Commonwealth of Australia.

- The shield in the centre represents the six states and federation.
- A kangaroo and an emu support the shield on each side. Kangaroos are native Australian animals, and emus are native Australian birds.
- A gold Commonwealth star sits above the shield.
- The background is the golden wattle, Australia's national flower.

National flower

Australia's national flower is the golden wattle. This small tree grows mainly in south-eastern Australia. It has bright green leaves and many golden-yellow flowers in spring and summer. Wattle Day is celebrated on 1 September each year. Each of the states and territories of Australia has its own floral emblem.

National colours

Australia's national colours are green and gold, the colours of the golden wattle. The uniforms of the national sports teams are usually green and gold.

National gemstone

The opal is Australia's national gemstone. According to Aboriginal legend, a rainbow touched the earth and created the colours of the opal.

National animal

The red kangaroo is the national animal. There are four main species of kangaroo in Australia, namely: the red kangaroo, the eastern grey kangaroo, the western grey kangaroo and the antilopine kangaroo. Red kangaroos are the biggest of the bunch and can be up to two metres in height and 90 kilograms in weight.

National bird

The emu (pronounced as "ee-myoo") is the second-largest living bird by height, after its relative, the ostrich. It is the largest native bird in Australia. The bird is sufficiently common for it to be rated as a least-concern species by the International Union for Conservation of Nature.

Emus are soft-feathered, brown, flightless birds with long necks and legs, and can reach up to 1.9 metres in height. Emus can travel great distances, and when necessary, can sprint at 50 km/h. They forage for a variety of plants and insects but have been known to go for weeks without eating.

The national anthem

The official national anthem - "Advance Australia Fair" consists of five verses. The anthem was officially adopted in 1984, and usually, the first two verses are sung.

We encourage you to teach the anthem to school-aged children. It is awkward for a child not to know the words the entire school is singing during assembly. More interesting facts about Australia can be downloaded from the Department of Home Affairs' Immigration and Citizenship Division: www.homeaffairs.gov.au

Advance Australia Fair

Australians all let us rejoice,
For we are young and free;
We've golden soil and wealth for toil;
Our home is girt by sea;
Our land abounds in nature's gifts
Of beauty rich and rare;
In history's page, let every stage
Advance Australia Fair.
In joyful strains then let us sing,
Advance Australia Fair.

Beneath our radiant Southern Cross
We'll toil with hearts and hands;
To make this Commonwealth of ours
Renowned of all the lands;
For those who've come across the seas
We've boundless plains to share;
With courage let us all combine
To Advance Australia Fair.
In joyful strains then let us sing,
Advance Australia Fair.

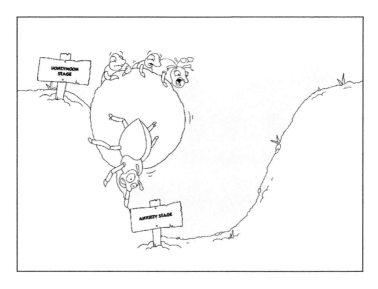

All immigrants experience culture shock when they arrive in their new adopted country. The first two stages are the Honeymoon stage, followed by the Anxiety stage.

3

PLANNING YOUR MOVE

"By failing to prepare, you are preparing to fail."

~ Benjamin Franklin
(American founding father, inventor, and diplomat)

There are so many scenarios and circumstances that can influence a move, that we could not possibly cover them all. But we can share our experiences and those of the hundreds of other people we have helped so that you can take the guesswork out of your move.

There are enough checklists on the internet of how and what to pack. We instead want to provide you with the insight and tools of how others have moved and how you can avoid common mistakes that can waste money.

We also want to give you information as to what is available to you here in Australia, so that you can plan effectively.

FIND YOUR "ANCHOR"

First, let's talk about a very fundamental part of the move, one we refer to several times in the book. To start your journey, you need a pivotal point, almost like that proverbial pin in the map that your new life will revolve around. We call it your "anchor".

What is the lifeline that you will throw down as your anchor in Australia? Is it a job? Is it a better education for your children, or is it a particular school? Your anchor could also be family or friends that are already living in Australia.

Whatever it is, there needs to be some point of reference from which everything else stems. Find your anchor and pivot your planning from there.

THE "LOOK-SEE-DECIDE" VISIT

The "look-see-decide" visit might be regarded as an unnecessary expense and perhaps even a gamble, but if timed correctly and planned well, it can have huge benefits and will save you a lot of money.

If you are organised and carry the operation out with precision, you might save thousands of dollars, so seriously consider it.

This visit also comes with a warning, though. It is often referred to as the "LSD trip" – look, see, decide (not the drug LSD). It has been given this name by many who have completed the trip, describing it as an event that passes quickly, and your eyes are wide open in shock the entire time!

Who to bring?

Don't bring the whole family, unless you are planning it as a holiday too. If it is just a look-see-visit, one adult with a list of things to do will suffice. However, we do recommend undertaking this as a couple, as you must work as a team from the beginning.

If only one half of the team has visited, the other spouse or partner can't always relate to what has been experienced during the visit, which could be problematic.

When is the best time?

There are two stages during the relocation that we would recommend you plan your visit:

1. The **constructive visit**, which is four to six weeks prior to your move.

2. The **exploration visit**, which is six months or more before your move.

The timing of your visit really can depend on various personal factors, especially your job situation, which might mean you have to visit for an interview anyway. Whichever one you choose, make sure that you are visiting towards the end of the week, as this is the best time to inspect rental properties. If you are lining up job interviews, then plan these meetings for a Monday, because real estate agents spend this day in the office processing weekend applications. You could also plan any other weekday morning for meetings or interviews. You will then be available in the afternoons and on Saturdays for rental property inspections.

The constructive visit

Around six to eight weeks before your move, you are in an excellent position to start making firm decisions. You will have to put actual plans in place for your arrival, to quicken your settling in time and save money.

You can also put yourself in a position to apply for rental properties and to attend job interviews if necessary. All of these will streamline your settling in period but will require military precision on your side to maximise the little time you have during the visit.

Having a home secured before your actual move is worth its weight in gold. The reasons for this are:

1. You have a **forwarding address** for mail.

2. You can **purchase a car** soon after your arrival.

3. The removalists have an **address** to supply to customs.

4. You will **save thousands** of dollars in temporary accommodation because now you can move directly into your own place.

5. You will have **ticked off** an important point on your immigration to-do list.

Making the most of the constructive visit is crucial to saving you money in the long run. If you are well-prepared, the advantages of this visit will outweigh the flight and accommodation costs. Having your house sorted will reduce your stress levels immensely.

It is worth hiring a **relocation consultant** to help orientate you and to help you to source and secure a rental property. The relocation consultant could continue to source properties for you once you have returned to home if you did not manage to complete the task during your short visit. Contact us if you need help from a professional relocation company at www.personnelrelocations.com.au

If you are not using a relocation consultant to help streamline and expedite your visit, make sure you have at least done the following:

1. You have **opened an Australian bank account** and deposited at least ten weeks' rent. You can open a bank account online and make deposits 28 days before your arrival.

2. After your arrival, you will need to go into the bank to **activate the account** so you can withdraw funds. The bank will only then start to prepare your cards.

3. To receive your cards, you will need a **postal address.** A friend's address or work address will suffice. This address is not proof of residence and needn't be your residential address.

4. You have **shortlisted the suburbs** you are interested in, to about a 10 to 20-kilometre radius of your anchor, or whatever has brought you to Australia.

5. Have **electronic copies** of your passport, visa, references, and anything else you need for job applications and rental applications ready (also refer to Chapter 16). We would recommend one paper copy – just in case!

6. Make sure you have read and familiarised yourself with the **rental inspection process** in Chapter 4.

7. **Hire a car** if you are visiting rental properties without a relocation consultant. With open inspections, you only have 15 minutes to view a home. Thus, you cannot rely on public transport to get around in time.

The exploration visit
If you are visiting Australia about six months to a year before your move, then it is to explore, to understand and help you relate to how things work in Australia. This type of visit has many benefits in helping you with your planning, and as we all know, knowledge is power. During this visit you could plan to tick off some of the following:

1. **Narrow down** the suburb(s) where you want to live.

2. Familiarise yourself with and use **public transport** to suburbs of interest.

3. **Book some school tours**, if nothing else, to familiarise yourself with the curriculum and possible differences. We recommend that you visit different types of schools, e.g. state and private schools.

4. Refer to **Chapters 4 and 5** before you embark on your exploration visit, to make sure you get the most out of it.

5. **Seek** out other groups who share a similar interest. These groups could be work, sport, hobbies or religious affiliations. Meeting people face-to-face and making real

connections will be helpful for advice and guidance, both during your visit.

6. A large portion of business in Australia is brought about by "word of mouth" and your "likability". **Connect with people**, use your contacts, and seek people with similar interests – that way, you already have something in common, which will be an ice breaker when you meet.

7. Seek people with **similar interests** in the following ways:
   - **LinkedIn:** Search by industry or by country.
   - **MeetUp groups:** Search by language, religion, hobbies and interests.
   - **Social media groups:** Search for Facebook groups such as Greeks/Polish living in Melbourne/Perth. There are usually groups for each suburb or neighbourhood too.

8. Activate your **driver's licence.** The process is simple but be aware that it can take up to two weeks to get an appointment. You can book online before your arrival. This is a bit of a catch 22-situation because you must provide proof of address, such as an invoice or any correspondence with your name and address on it. If you have opened your bank account using a friend's address, then this will be displayed on your bank statement, and this address can be used to apply for your driving licence. Your licence will be posted to your home address.

Top tip: *If you are visiting far in advance of your actual move and you have been granted permanent residency (PR), then you must obtain your Australian driver's licence. In most states, a person who is granted PR has six months from the time they enter the country to change their driver's licence.*

9. Find a **relocation consultant** to assist you with your migration journey - www.personnelrelocations.com.au Remember, you are not only engaging a professional, but also someone who knows the local schools and suburbs.

This person will have the best tips on saving you and your family money and significantly reducing your stress levels.

10. Plan your trip according to the **best times for open inspections** on Saturdays. The best time to fly to Australia is early in the week, like on a Sunday or Monday.

To make the most of your visit, keep this book handy as a guideline and connect with us on social media to stay updated.

Understand the Australian culture before you make assumptions or have any pre-conceived ideas. Collect store advertisements, catalogues, and other relevant documents for show-and-tell when you return home. Take lots of notes and photos.

MOVING YOUR PETS

What to do with your pets is a very emotional decision. It is difficult to leave a pet behind, even if you find it the best new home. We do sympathise, but you must give the decision careful consideration.

Factors to consider are the costs, which is around the same price usually, like that of an adult's Business Class air travel. If you are coming from a Rabies-infected country, then the six-month preparation time for the animal in your home country is a consideration as this could severely delay your departure.

You must also consider how well your pet might travel. It will be in a crate for an extended period of time. If it is nervous by nature, then it is probably kinder to leave it in someone else's care at home. Pets that are already hiding from thunder and lightning will suffer at an airport with worse noises and nowhere to hide. It can be very traumatic for them. Consider their age.

Remember, you are moving to a "Rabies-free" country, and Australia is determined to keep it that way. If you want to bring your pets, we can't stress enough how important it is to start the process early and stick to the plan.

Immunisations and blood tests are all planned in a time-sensitive way. If you miss any of these dates, you will have to start the whole process all over again. Make sure you are working with a veterinarian (vet) who knows the process.

Please don't consider sending your pet with just any supplier. Make sure you check up on and research the pet carrier first. Check on the regulations and the care your pet will receive during a stopover, as your pet will be taken off the aeroplane. Some countries do not have the love and respect for pets that we do. We could have taken another 20 pages of this book to lay out the steps to relocate your pet, but The Department of Agriculture and Water Resources (DAWR) has a very detailed and up-to-date website where you can investigate this matter thoroughly:

www.agriculture.gov.au/cats-dogs

Cost-saving tip: *Make sure that the quarantine facility in Australia is booked well in advance. If you are using a reputable pet carrier, they usually have booking slots already allocated. If you are moving the pet yourself, note that quarantine stations are only in Melbourne and Sydney (discussions are underway to close Sydney). Failure to book early will result in additional costs to ship your pet interstate.*

WHAT TO BRING AND WHAT NOT TO BRING TO AUSTRALIA?

Electrical goods or appliances

In Australia, the standard voltage is 230V, and the frequency is 50Hz. If your electrical items are the same, you may only need to change your plugs. If not, you will require a converter, which can be troublesome.

Consider the age of your appliances, generally speaking, if it is over five-eight years, it might not survive a long sea journey.

It is also advisable to check if the brands of your white-goods are available in Australia; otherwise, you may not find a repairer or parts should it break down. You will limit your rental accommodation options if you have a large or double door fridge that cannot fit into the kitchen space.

Cars/motorbikes

Taking a car or motorbike to Australia is not recommended unless the vehicle is a classic and valuable. Even then, give it serious consideration.

Imported cars are subject to sales tax based on the replacement value of the vehicle in Australia (not the value in your home country). You must make sure the car is thoroughly steam cleaned for quarantine, and remember, there is a lot of paperwork to be completed on both sides of the world.

Once your vehicle has finally arrived in Australia, you will have further delays while you wait for its safety and emission checks, registration, and roadworthiness certificate. Let's also not forget the cost of the actual transportation of the car. You will have to decide if all this is worthwhile.

Fire-arms

The Port Arthur massacre took place in 1996 when the gunman opened fire on shop owners and tourists with two semi-automatic rifles. The massacre left 35 people dead and 23 wounded. This mass killing horrified the Australian public and transformed gun control legislation in Australia.

A person must have a fire-arm licence to possess or use a firearm. Licence holders must demonstrate a "genuine reason" (which does not include self-defence) for holding a fire-arm licence and must not be a "prohibited person".

All firearms must be registered by serial number to an owner with a fire-arm licence. It is not a simple process to import your fire-arm, and generally, people do not bring them into the country. It is such an involved procedure with many visits to the state police control centre.

REPLACING COST OF FURNITURE AND WHITE GOODS

In Australia, we have a variety of shops providing different levels of "comfort and luxury" or "cheap and cheerful". Also, refer to Chapter 6. For most people, "cheap and cheerful" is a good start to reduce outlay costs and get started.

Second-hand shops are not typical in Australia, but if you look on Gumtree and Facebook Marketplace, you will find well-priced second-hand furniture. The Freecycle Network® offers free second-hand furniture and goods.

We also have several charity shops, where you can pick up some smaller items. Don't look down on charity shops – called "op shops", short for "opportunity". Australians donate excellent quality goods and also brand new, unopened goods, still in the original packaging. Again, refer to Chapter 6 for more on "op shops".

Some of the Australian shops you can research online to obtain comparative or replacement items:
1. **Freedom Furniture:** Mid-price range of furniture and accessories.
2. **IKEA:** Tiered price range on all items, as well as starter sets for pots, pans, crockery.
3. **Kmart:** A little like Game and Mr Price rolled into one.
4. **Amart Furniture:** Basic furniture that will see you through for a few years.
5. **Fantastic Furniture:** Basic furniture that will see you through for a few years.
6. **Koala Mattresses:** An online Australian favourite with a free 100-day trial.
7. **Harvey Norman:** An Aussie icon for furniture and appliances.
8. **The Good Guys:** All appliances from fridges to hair driers.
9. **Appliances Online:** All appliances and a good comparison site.
10. **Snooze:** Beds and bedroom suites.
11. **Forty Winks:** Beds and bedroom suites.

Note: *In Australia, most furniture can arrive as flat-packed items. You will have to assemble the items yourself with the tools that are included in your flat pack. IKEA, Freedom and other shops do offer an "assembly service" for a fee. There are also other companies you can engage in* *building flat-packs if you have to furnish an entire house. In most instances, it does take two people to build a flat-pack item. Read the instructions before you start and make sure all the pieces are in the box.*

Real-life story

Between IKEA and KMART, we furnished a two-bedroom apartment for a client for under $3 000.00 (2018) She was an engineer working on a wind farm and had to shop online. She chose all the items, saved the lists, and we just collected and placed them in the apartment before her arrival. That included everything from beds, glasses, pots and pans, a sofa, and even the dishtowels!

FURNITURE REMOVALS

Time is money when you are in transit. Your removals can be one of your most significant expenses. Hidden costs are likely, where you will be wasting money while your goods are being shipped.

The longer you are without your personal belongings, the more money you will be wasting on fast food and accommodation. You need to give this lots of thought and due consideration. Please don't opt for "cheap and cheerful" removalists!

The only time you want to get a "cheap and cheerful" removalist quote is to assess what the lowest price might be and to use this to ask your preferred removalist to sharpen the pencil. Don't expect a reputable, accredited removalist to meet that price. However, there is always room to improve on price.

SHIPPING

Sharing a container

If you are looking for the most economical way to send your goods, and you do not have a large volume, you could opt to share a container, called "LCL" or "Groupage". We only recommend this if you have friends or family you can live with while your goods are in transit.

The shared container will only leave the harbour when it is full. This option will increase your shipping time by anything from 3-8 weeks. If you are seriously considering this option, then choose a larger moving company who is always busy. They will have more containers going on the same track you need.

Shipping container sizes
Standard ISO shipping containers are 8 feet (2.43 m) wide and 8.5 feet (2.59 m) high. They come in two lengths:
- 20 feet (6.06 m) and
- 40 feet (12.2 m).

Top tip: *Measure this space out in your garage and mark it with chalk to get a visual of how big it is.*

Moving Cubes®
There is another option that requires more manual labour on your behalf, but it is cheaper. Some companies can deliver moving crates, which you then pack yourself and they will ship them. There are usually three different sizes of wooden crates. You pack all of your boxes and have everything in your garage. They will come and pack the goods into your wooden crate, which is placed in a sea container and shipped. You are responsible for your contents, so the risk is on you not to pack any banned items. Seven Seas are kept busy, so we are finding excellent transit times with them, as opposed to groupage where they can't ship the container until it is full.

Airfreight
Airfreight is the most costly option, but of course, the quickest way to send anything that you will need soon after your arrival and that you don't want to haul through the airport.

We mention airfreight in Chapter 14 when we discuss budgets. As explained, airfreight cost is influenced more by the weight of the items, than their size. Airfreight gets packed on air pallets, or sometimes even enclosed in a large plastic container that fits onto a pallet.

The advantage of sending your goods with a removalist, instead of using excess luggage or freight forward, is that the removalist will keep your consignment together, so there is less chance of one carton box not arriving. Removalists will wrap your boxes up together to fit them all on one pallet or container. Try to keep airfreight to around four to six standard carton boxes. A standard carton box is 40 cm x 40 cm x 60 cm.

That does not mean you can't put something like a pram in airfreight; the box size is a guide only. Your airfreight should be essential items that you may need while you are in temporary accommodation or that will help you if you find a rental quickly and want to move in and "camp".

Don't be fooled into thinking your airfreight will arrive at the same time as you. It will arrive around a week later. Anything you will desperately need within that week; you will have to take on the aeroplane with you. Airfreight can only leave after you have left, and it usually takes a couple of days to clear customs and quarantine, then organise a delivery slot to your residence.

If you are choosing to spend $3 000 on airfreight, it must be things you will need, according to your personal preference. Maybe you want silk pillowcases, or you need some toys for the children. Here are some further thoughts, ideas, and prompts to consider adding to your airfreight consignment:

1. A **multi-plug**, with an international adaptor - you can use the adaptor to plug the multi-plug in, and the rest of the sockets are available for your home country appliances. One for mobile devices in the lounge area and one for the kitchen if you are taking any small appliances. Please note this is a safety hazard, so it should only be a temporary solution.

2. An **electric frying pan** or you can also buy them in Australia for around $30 at Kmart. No matter what short term accommodation you have, those pans are always too small to cook a packet of mince or more than three

burger patties. If you are staying at a caravan park, then this pan is worth its weight in gold. Motels do not offer cooking facilities and are therefore not insured for fires caused by cooking. If you burn the place down, you will be liable for the damage.

3. **Linen and pillows** are things most people put in airfreight (vacuum wrap them to save space). This is an excellent idea when you have children. It is especially comforting for children if they can sleep on their own, familiar linen. Other items for children might include a few small toys and a night lamp and their "usual" set of plates or cutlery.

4. If your children are starting school immediately, then **immunisation records** and **black school shoes** are things you may be bringing. But consider if the airfreight will arrive in time for the start of school.

Real-life story

A French client sent all his camping gear by airfreight. He had a little foldout table, two chairs, an inflatable mattress, a sleeping bag and some linen. His coffee machine, basic plastic crockery and larger knives than you would find in a hotel, were also part of the deal. For him, it worked because he did not have time to go out and buy these items. However, we still think you could rather buy them in Australia for less than the cost of airfreight.

CHOOSING A MOVING COMPANY

The removals process can start around 18 months before you leave. Research and read reviews about companies, ask for recommendations and do whatever you can to narrow down the list to at least three to five removalists.

Then check the following: Do they have accreditation? Do they belong to an association of removalists who are responsible for their standards and code of conduct? You are moving internationally, so local accreditation is not always enough. As a guide, try to use removalists who are accredited by the following organisations:

1. **FIDI** (Fédération Internationale des Déménageurs Internationaux) – The most established global alliance of professional international moving and relocation companies with a strict code of conduct. Companies are audited every three years: www.fidi.org/find-fidi-affiliate

2. **BAR** – British Association of Removers, or the International Association of Movers: www. bar.co.uk/why-use-a-bar-member-for-your-move/

3. **AFRA** – Australian Furniture Removers Association – does not have international recognition but still has acceptable standards: www.afra.com.au/find-a-removalist-2/

Do your shortlisted removalists have offices in Australia? If they have local offices, this can be helpful when you are waiting for delivery in Australia, and you want to phone someone locally.

We also find that there are fewer insurance debates if you have the same company collecting in your home country and delivering in Australia. There is no argument over who is to blame because it's the same company.

Never, ever choose a removalist who works with online inventory quotes. These companies will ask you to enter all your furniture and other items online, and they send you a quote. This option is a winning recipe for disaster. If someone has not physically inspected your home, they could arrive on the arranged date, to discover you need a shuttle vehicle into your estate. They will add more money, and you will have no alternative but to pay. Physical inspections for quotes are a must.

After you made a shortlist, it is time to call and organise inspections with the removal companies. Each inspection should take around an hour. Feel free to schedule them directly after each other in one afternoon. However, do not have them all at the same time. You want to be able to get a feel for each company by interacting with them on an individual basis.

Real-life story

When we moved from France to Australia, I was bowled over by the wonderful marketing of a particular company. They promised to colour code the bedrooms with the boxes and pack the kitchen stuff last. None of this made any difference when on moving day, they arrived with the wrong sized container. It was a complete nightmare. It was also the move where we had the most breakages than any of our other moves across the globe. Half of our belongings were packed into a truck and then packed into a container at a warehouse where it was left unsupervised.

Note: *Make sure the excellent service doesn't end as soon as you have signed on the dotted line.*

PREPARING FOR YOUR REMOVALS INSPECTIONS

You *must* be at home for the inspections. We can't tell you how many migrants leave this meeting to their housekeepers or elderly family members or relatives to oversee. Not only are some things forgotten, such as failing to show the estimator the garage or tool-shed, but critical information is also shared about customs and quarantine.

You must be present at this meeting. If the estimator just leaves paperwork for you to read, you might not go through them, or they might not make sense. This is a costly part of your move, where you want to trust who is going to look after your worldly goods. If you are going to compare removalists, you need to know what they offer.

The quoting process can start a year in advance. If you are sending items by both air and sea freight, try to separate the two so the estimator can see the volume. Alternatively, ask all the estimators to quote on four to six standard carton boxes. You want all of them to quote on the same volume.

When the salesperson/estimator arrives at your home for the inspection, be mindful not to be bowled over by the wonderful sales tactics that you are about to experience. These companies put a lot of money into their marketing.

By all means, enjoy the process, but stay focused and look out for the following tactics. The estimators usually have worked for the opposition, and they will ask you who else you are getting in to quote. They know the intricate details of the opposition, including their cost methods and quote layouts, and will consider the opposition when they quote because usually, the lowest price wins, right?

If you are asked who else is quoting, feel free to say who, but also feel free to ask if they know the company and what you should "be aware of". This question can often give you some pointers as to what to look out for in general.

The last thing you want on moving day is that your stuff is collected and then the removalist starts adding to the costs by saying that certain things were not included. At that stage, you will be at their mercy. You will be stressed, emotionally drained and will have nothing else to do but hand over the credit card. Attention to detail on the quotes is therefore essential.

Prepare yourself for the inspection and be armed with questions and know how you would like your quotes to be laid out, so you can easily compare apples with apples.

QUESTIONS TO ASK THE SALES ESTIMATOR

Packers and movers

Make sure whether the company employs the packing team or if they are contract workers. Many moving companies use a man who owns a truck and hires some day labourers.

You don't want this, not in your home country and not in Australia! Packing teams that are employed by the removalist will have regular police checks, received proper training and adhere to company policies and procedures.

Shipping timelines

The removalists might tell you that your goods will travel about six to eight weeks at sea (depending on your distance from Australia). This is true, but what they don't tell you is the time on land and in the harbour, either side of the globe.

Think about it, where is the nearest harbour to your home? Your goods still need to get from your doorstep to the harbour where they could wait for a few days for the next freight ship. When the goods arrive in Australia, it takes time to clear customs and quarantine. We recommend you add another two weeks on each side of the world as a good buffer.

Shipping vessels all follow the same shipping lines around the coast, but some vessels might stop more often than others. It is essential to know the shipping times so that you can accurately work out a budget for your temporary accommodation schedule.

We can assure you that nothing under five weeks is possible. Don't be caught by the sales jargon. If you know the vessel name, you can track the ship at sea, which is also fun for kids to do.

There are several websites you can use for this, like www.vesselfinder.com and www.myshiptracking.com

Packing timelines

The packing timelines are essential information as you need to know how long the packaging process will take.

It is common courtesy to inform your neighbours or security guards, if applicable, about your move and that there may be a large container truck parked in the road.

You also need to know how much time you will have to clean the house and provide the keys to the new owner or real estate agent. Most international moves take about two to three days to be packed. The first (and second) day they will wrap and crate everything, and by the second day, they will start to pack the container.

Terms of payment

Concerning the payment, consider asking the removalists the following questions:

1. **How much** is due to secure the date?

2. Does every cent have to be **paid in advance**?

3. Can you get a **fixed price**? No matter what they find on move day, the company will be obliged to stick to the quoted price.

Shipment delivery in Australia

There are very few removalists who have offices in both your home country and Australia. It is worth the effort to find such a company, as it will give you some peace of mind because both offices will be using the same level of service.

Communication during a move is essential, and when your move is orchestrated by one company, it allows for clear communication, as everyone is on the same page.

Offices in both countries can make insurance claims easier too, without too much of a blame game when you are dealing with the same company.

If you are considering a removalist who will contract the work out to another removalist in Australia, you want to know everything about the Australian company too. Their service and reputation require just as much of your attention as your local company.

Paperwork

Make sure that all the quotes include the necessary paperwork as well. Import permits and customs and quarantine clearances should be included. Check that all the quotes include the full processing of your container through the ports. Most quotes will include this, but if a removalist is trying to reduce some costs to appear competitive, they may omit to do this. You want a fully inclusive door-to-door service.

Accreditation

As mentioned before, don't conduct an international move with a company who does not hold some sort of international accreditation or belong to an international association, to whom they are responsible for their standards and processes.

Be sure to check that the company in Australia is also an accredited moving company. There are many "fly-by-night" operators out there. You want a company who has its own vehicles and crew; not a company contracted out to some rogue operator.

COMPARING QUOTES

A sales estimator who does not ask you who else you are getting quotes from is probably not doing his job well. They are asking so they know where to pitch their job! To make it easier for you to compare "apples with apples" on your removal quotes, we would recommend you ask each removalist to present the quote with the following details in an easy to find format.

Volume of shipment

You want the same unit of measurement on all the quotes, so you can easily compare quotes at a glance – and more importantly, so you can ensure they have all measured and quoted on the same volume. This might vary slightly, but there should not be a vast difference. We have reviewed quotes where a removalist left out the entire garage, another where all the garden furniture was omitted. Being able to see the cubic meters easily will show you quickly if they have forgotten something.

Itemised costs

Removalist quotes generally cover ground and first-floor moves. If you are living in a house that has steps to the front door and steps again inside the house, this could be deemed a second floor.

If you live in an estate, make sure the removals truck can

access your home easily; otherwise, a shuttle vehicle might be required.

You want to see these costs itemised separately. They can be used as a bargaining tool when you want to negotiate the price too. You also want to make sure everything has been included in the quote. Never assume an estimator has remembered everything, you want to see it in black and white.

Shipping and transportation timelines
You want to easily compare the shipping times and hold the company to ransom if they don't adhere to this further down the line.

Packing and wrapping
There are some ways that companies use to cut their costs. Packing material is one way to save on costs, so make sure you have a clear picture and understanding of how your belongings will be wrapped and packed.

Special packing and crating
Special packing and crating costs are extra. If one removalist has omitted to quote for crating your 65-inch television, then their quote will immediately look cheaper.

Make sure you know what these types of items cost in Australia, to decide if they are worth moving or not. You will not be comparing quotes equally if they are not all quoting on the same items.

Insurance
Insurance is a necessary evil. Now, this is one of those costs that is well hidden in removalists' quotes, because it is shown innocently as a percentage and it is rarely included in the overall amount on your quote. It should be between 2.5% and 3.5% - anything more is excessive.

The insurance is based on the value you place on your personal belongings. If you place a value of $90 000 on your goods being shipped, approximately another $3 000 will be added to your quote for insurance. Depending on the percentage quoted, and on your estimated value, this can seriously impact your quotes. Be sure to compare this percentage between your quotes.

The insurance excess amount is also worth comparing. An excess of $50 000 is not of much use when they have broken every dinner plate! An excess of $1 000 to $2 500 is usually enough, but it is a personal preference. If you negotiate a lower excess, expect to pay a higher insurance premium.

Also, make sure to check the fine print, sometimes the excess is only valid on items above a certain value, or on itemised items.

Another word of caution:

Please check who is underwriting the insurance. Is it a reputable company? The insurance should not be "covered" by the removalists themselves. This is not only non-compliant but leaves you at risk if the company should go insolvent. This sadly does happen.

When we are managing the removalists, we arrange insurance with Australian based insurers. This also makes it much easier to claim for any breakages, rather than trying to claim it from your home country when you are already in Australia. You will not get any sympathy from any insurance company when you have left your home country.

Companies such as **Removal Management Worldwide** (www.rmww.com.au), can obtain three independent quotes for your move, and they provide Australian-based insurance.

Real-life story

A lady who moved to Melbourne thought her strategy of using a cheap removalist with plenty of insurance was a great plan. The cheap removalist was using a shipping line that "stops at all ports", so it would take longer.

Insured to the hilt, she got a call after a few weeks to say the removalist had "gone under". The removalist hadn't paid the shipping company, and her container was subsequently offloaded in Brisbane.

As it was "illegally portsided", she incurred $800 per day in fines by the port authorities. Her container would only be released once the bill was paid. It had already been portsided for eight days before they had found her contact details to call her! As the removalist had gone under, she had also lost all her insurance.

SUMMARY OF RECOMMENDATIONS

1. Carefully consider what furniture you will be moving.

2. Consider how you will move everything: sea freight, excess luggage, air freight etc.

3. Make a shortlist of companies based on your criteria.

4. Be present at the inspection and ask the estimator lots of questions. He or she will be surprised at how well organised you are!

5. Each company needs to quote in the same format so you can easily compare apples with apples. A template for comparing removalist quotes:

Items to compare	Quote 1	Quote 2	Quote 3
Price - sea			
Price - air			
Time at sea			
Volume quoted on			
Insurance %			
Accredited with FIDI/BAR			
Company in Australia			
Itemised pieces special packing/shuttle vehicle 1. 2. 3.			
My customer service rating			
Payment terms			

6. The longer you are without your belongings, the more money you will be spending on temporary accommodation and fast food and the higher your stress levels will be.

7. Check the insurance. Who underwrites it? What is the excess? How does one claim? What is excluded? If there are exclusions such as jewellery, then make sure it is covered by your personal travel insurance.

4

A ROOF OVER YOUR HEAD

"Look at the birds of the air:
They do not sow or reap or gather into barns -
and yet your Heavenly Father feeds them.
Are you not much more valuable than they?"

~ Matthew 6: 27 (NIV)

It can seem overwhelming to decide where in Australia you are going to live. The million-dollar question is: Where do you start?

Australia is a very big country with so many options. In fact, Australia is the world's biggest island and smallest continent. It is approximately 3 700 kilometres from North to South and 4 000 kilometres from East to West. It is twenty times bigger than Japan, fourteen times bigger than France and 2.4 times bigger than India.

Narrowing down your search to about a 20-kilometre radius suddenly seems like a huge task, and it is, but we are here to guide you. Our experience is your foresight. Take a deep breath – it will be okay.

We use the following questions to ascertain important information from any new arrivals. You can use the same method to narrow down your search for a place to call home.

WHAT IS YOUR ANCHOR?

We have already explained this in Chapter 3. An anchor is what we refer to as the only definite, the concrete pillar or the proverbial pin on the map that everything revolves around; in other words, your starting point. This could be a workplace, a particular school, where friends or family are already living, or a religious affiliation.

REASON(S) FOR MOVING

This could be the same as your anchor, but not necessarily so. Some people arrive in Australia with no job, no family or friends. You have moved thousands of miles to be in Australia. What was your motivation? Was it for quality education and a better future for your children? Then you need to start by narrowing down your school choices.

Lifestyle

Maybe you want to live close to the beach, or perhaps you want to be able to cycle to work. Maybe you are a trail runner and would prefer to be close to the hills. Or you want to live in a remote area (suburb) which is still close to a train station.

Budget

Yes, everything comes down to the budget in the end. What rent can you afford? What cost of living can you afford? Maybe you will have two cars, or you might prefer to have only one car and also use public transport. You will have to figure out where you can save money and where you can compromise to be able to find a balance between your lifestyle and your budget.

Real-life story

A few years ago, we met an ex-pat family. After taking advice from the Human Resources Department at the husband's company, they settled in an affluent suburb that was convenient for work and access to the city but was 60 kilometres from their place of worship where they wanted to join their religious community.

With the various children's activities at the place of worship, they were undertaking the 60 kilometres trip, three times a week. It is all good and well to live in an affluent suburb where your kids attend a "posh" private school, but when your anchor, support network and daily needs are far away, it is not such a good idea anymore.

Temporary accommodation

Besides the furniture removals, temporary accommodation will be your biggest expense. While you are in "limbo" you will be experiencing costs that you hadn't planned for, like extra meals on the run and parking and internet costs.

Convenience has to be your focus! We cannot stress this enough. It all comes back to what we were saying about having an "anchor". What has brought you to Australia? A job, school, family? Your temporary accommodation should be near to whatever your "anchor" is. This should, if possible, coincide with where you will be house hunting because you can't always control the time that you can inspect rental properties. You may find that you have to visit one property at 10am and another property at 5pm.

Being close to your search area will be an important benefit. By living in temporary accommodation close to or within your search area, is also a way to familiarise yourself with your new surroundings. The first few weeks is usually characterised by an information overload, and you will be acutely aware of what is going on around you. Convenience also means that you should be close to groceries and local services. Temporary accommodation does not usually provide a lot of fridge space. Don't be surprised if you will be hauling grocery bags every other day.

People tend to overthink their temporary accommodation. Try to have a budget in mind and go with it. Don't think about it too much. It is only for a few weeks, just be rational about it. We have seen migrants spending hours drooling over temporary accommodation. Think with your head and not your heart in this instance.

Choosing a suburb

Despite your best efforts, and no matter how hard you try, real estate agents won't give you the time of day until you arrive in Australia, money in hand and ready to move in.

When you are still in your home country, keep watching the rental market though, familiarise yourself with how quickly properties might be moving in your targeted area, which agents are active, and start building a benchmark of what is "normal".

This advice comes with a warning, though. What you see on the internet is not always what you get in real life. Real estate agents can use old photos, enhance photos or just hide any sore eyes. For examples of such cases visit the blogs on www.personnelrelocations.com.au/blog/

It does not surprise us when we arrive at an advertised home that looks bright and white on the internet, and the agent opens the door to salmon pink carpets and lime green wallpaper. No jokes!

The hardest part is knowing what to do first. Sometimes, without knowing the process, you can find yourself in a catch-22 situation. If you are not using a relocation consultant, narrowing down your search area can be difficult. You can ask around at work, but your Aussie colleagues all love where they live and will sing their own suburb's praises loudly. This may leave you a bit confused.

Alan, the guy with the buttoned cardigan and beard, loves the vibrancy of his neighbourhood and the sound of the coffee shops and wine bars. But is this a place to bring up children?

Sophia, the sophisticated executive assistant with three children, loves the open spaces and play areas in her suburb, but will it fit in with your budget?

A different approach is to ask the already settled migrants in Australia for advice or just copy what they have done. Remember, it may have worked well for them, but is this going to suit you and your family? You may find yourself saying: "Oh dear, but their children don't play the same sport. We will need to get to hockey games on the other side of town."

A good relocation consultant knows the areas and can help you consider your particular circumstance and suggest a suitable suburb. Just a few hours with a consultant will get you on the right track. Okay, you have identified your anchor. What happens now? Below are a few pointers to help you shortlist your search area.

What will be your mode of transportation?

Will you drive to work, use public transport, walk or maybe even cycle? What is a comfortable commute time for you? Use the "Directions" function in Google Maps to ascertain distance, different routes, and travel times.

Public transportation in Australia is reliable and safe. You can access the public transport website, for the city you will be moving to, online. They also have very user-friendly mobile apps that can be downloaded to plan your commute. Keep in mind that there are more travel options during peak times. For example, a train may run every eight minutes into the city between 7am and 9am, but then only every 20 minutes for the rest of the day.

Budget is always a consideration

Several factors can influence the price of a rental property. When you are sitting in your home country with your wish list for the new home, you may be surprised and confused by the variance in rents in a specific area.

What will everyday life be like for you?

Besides a work commute, will there be after school activities or work commitments? You might want to live close to the beach, which is great, but how often will you go to the beach? If it's only once a week, then it is not a priority to live close to the sea. That said, you will most likely drive to the beach anyway, so is an extra five minutes such a big deal?

If religion is a significant part of your life, then this is a great place to start your search. Find the place of worship (see Chapter 6 for websites) you want to attend and contact them via email. Enquire where your fellow countrymen are living (usually a selection of suburbs) and then ask which schools their children are attending. The office at your intended place of worship will most probably provide you with contact details of some of these families.

After our relocation consultant assisted us with finding a rental property and connecting all the utilities, we were overwhelmed by the help from the local Australians through our church. We couldn't have asked for a softer landing and more positive start.

Like anywhere in the world, the closer to the city you are, the higher the rent and the less space you might have around you. The further away from the city, the more you can get for your money, such as bigger bedrooms, a bigger garden and double garages. The same can be said for the period houses versus the modern builds – the older the house, the bigger the rooms.

In Melbourne, for example, if you live 45 minutes from the inner city, a four-bedroom house with double garage and garden costs about the same as a two-bedroom apartment in Port Melbourne (eight minutes from the city). The same can be said for those sea or city views. If you want proximity to the beach and a view, be prepared to pay a little more.

Migrants who are not used to safe, reliable public transport, and an abundance of transport options, will probably not consider public transport as a priority. If you are moving with children, though, you will want to be within walking distance to public transportation. This convenience can add to your rental price. But on the upside, you will save money on buying, registering, insuring and running a motor vehicle. It will also be helpful in the early days before you buy a car, or maybe it will eliminate the need for a second car.

It is fair to say that, although the proximity to public transport will add around $10/$20 per week to your rental price, you will save that two-fold in car costs.

Schools can influence the rental prices in some suburbs. Schools listed as top state schools will attract families to those catchment zones. Obviously, it can vary depending on the time of year. Around January, the start of the school year, there is a much higher demand, which can inflate prices during this time. This concerns only state schools, as only state schools have catchment zones. You don't have to worry about catchment zones if you are considering private or semiprivate schools. If the school has available space and you have the money, they will take your child.

Real-life story
A French family we relocated had four school-aged children. The father was a tri-athlete and needed to cycle at least 30 km every day. This was their "anchor". We found a suburb within 15 km from his office and a highly sought-after local school.

VISITING RENTAL PROPERTIES
You narrowed down your search area by using the www.realestate.com.au or www.domain.com.au websites to create a shortlist. A useful feature on these websites is the creation of custom searches. Your searches for different areas will be saved and are easily accessible again when you need to consider a specific suburb. This feature saves time, and you can add your email address to receive updates on a daily or weekly basis as new properties are listed.

There are two ways to inspect a property:

1. **Private inspection,** where you phone the estate agent, and he or she is willing to come out and show you through the home.

2. **Open for inspection (OFI)** is where there is an advertised inspection time on the internet. The real estate agent only goes out once to open the door for everyone who wants to see the home. Then the agent returns to the office and waits for the flurry of applications!

With OFI's, the front door will be open for the advertised time only, usually 15 minutes. You can arrive anytime during that time, but the door will be closed, and you will be asked to leave at the end of the advertised time.

Usually, the OFI is not hosted by the property manager responsible for the property. It might be an agent who is on duty that day for all the open inspections in the area. This person will have a bunch of keys and a list of open times. The person literally just goes from one property to another, and that is why you need to leave on time.

What implications does this have for you? You needn't wear your best suit, or try to overly impress this agent, as he or she may have no say in your application. Always be polite, though – it goes without saying! Casual dress is acceptable, but we draw the line at wearing thongs (flip flops). Be presentable, be casual, and just don't be scruffy.

The assigned agent will usually just stand at the door for the duration of your inspection. You will not be introduced to each room but will have to make your own way through the property. Don't hand this agent your application, unless you have spoken and confirmed that, that is the person who will handle your application.

With a private inspection, keep it to around 15-20 minutes, depending on the size of the property. Focus on the floorplan (most advertised properties will have a floorplan you can download). Is it going to work for you and your family? This is not the time to check that every window opens, and the taps are working, but ensuring the home is functional and structurally safe.

Once you move into a property, you will have three business days to complete a property condition report, where you will have time to check for leaky taps or squeaky windows. If during an inspection, you notice something which is totally unacceptable, like a door hanging off its hinges, you can state that on your application. You may ask for it to be fixed before accepting the property. Ask the estate agent if the door will be repaired. If you don't get a clear answer, by all means, put it on your application.

We say this with caution, though. Be realistic and remember that you don't want to look like a "high maintenance" applicant. Applications are all about the opposition – who else is applying, is their application stronger than yours? If you have a list of demands, your application will quickly be put at the bottom of the pile.

What to look for when you only have 15 minutes?

Quickly walk through the property to check the floorplan – does it have all the rooms you need? Then start again, this time checking:

1. **Bathrooms:** Is there proper ventilation? If no window, is there an extraction fan? If you prefer a bath, is there one? You will be surprised how easy it is to miss something you expect to be there.

2. **Bedrooms:** Open the cupboards – are there drawers inside or do they only have hanging space? This is not a deal-breaker, but it is good to know for your preparation. IKEA sells wardrobe inserts.

3. **Kitchen:** Is there a dishwasher, oven, and cooktop (cooker/stove)? Is it a gas, induction, or electric cooktop? Is there an extraction fan? Open a few drawers and cupboards just to make sure they work okay. If you don't have a tape measure handy, then step into the fridge compartment to get an idea of its size.

4. **Laundry:** Where are the laundry taps located? Will the washing machine be underneath a counter? If so, you will need a front-loading machine, not a top loader.

5. **Garage:** Any roof leaks? Is the door remote controlled?

6. **Garden:** Is the garden private or can the neighbours see what you are doing? If it is a manicured garden, ask if garden maintenance is included.

7. **Central heating and cooling** are popular in Australia, and many migrants are not used to the convenience of ducted heating and cooling. Another way to heat or cool a home is with wall mounted units known as a "split system" (air conditioner and usually heating). Ducted central heating and cooling is the most effective system. It is also usually the most economical to run because the heating is fuelled by gas and the split system by electricity.

Top tip: *You should make your own little checklist of what is important to you beforehand. Take this list with you because not only is it practical, but it will also help you think with your head and not with your heart. The property needs to be practical and suitable for the first year at least, but it must also have a homely feel.*

When you are inspecting the property, check the following:

1. If you think the house has had rooms added, check that there are heating and cooling in those rooms too. Some homes might only have heating and cooling in the new part of the house, not throughout the home. If you are not sure about the vents, ask the agent, some heating vents are in the floor, and cooling vents in the ceiling.

2. When you read a rental advert, and it says, "split systems", then you already know that the whole house is not heated and cooled. Split systems are usually installed in the lounge, and hopefully also cools the kitchen area.

3. If you have bedrooms upstairs, make sure there are cooling units upstairs – hot air rises, and there is nothing worse than trying to sleep when it is hot!

4. If it is an older property, with high ceilings, chances are

you will need heating. Often bathrooms are heated by "heating globes". Check this, especially if you are going to live in Victoria, Tasmania, South Australia and Canberra and have children who will be bathing – you will definitely want some heating in the bathrooms.

THE APPLICATION PROCESS

Your application is the "offer" that you are making to the landlord via the property manager (real estate agent). Always try to put your best offer on the table.

The process works as follows:

1. **Visit the property**, either by private appointment or OFI.

2. **Submit your application.** Remember, the real estate agent can take anything from one hour to three days to come back to you.

3. The real estate agent will **shortlist three applications** to be presented to the landlord.

4. The **landlord** ultimately decides who gets the property.

5. The **real estate agent** will usually phone to inform you that your application has been approved and will ask if you are still interested in the property.

6. You will then be **emailed a confirmation letter**, which includes detail like how to pay your first month's rent.

7. You have **24 hours** from the time of notice of approval, to pay the rent, or the property will be offered to the next shortlisted applicant.

8. You can apply for **more than one property at a time**, as long as you or your representative has visited the property. The rental market works very quickly here, and if you wait three days for an application to be approved, you have already missed out on other homes. The estate agents understand this, and it is for this reason that they will phone you to check if you are still interested in renting the

house, before they put it in writing with the confirmation email.

To familiarise yourself with the rental application process, you should take a look at the 1Form-application. This is an online application that around 80% of the estate agents use. The 1Form is the most comprehensive, so any other form you are presented with will be a breeze to complete. Using the 1Form, you can complete all the personal details of your application, upload your supporting documents, and save them. Once you have visited a property, you can take five minutes to insert the address of the property and submit your application online, super-fast!

In the first instance, Australians work on a "first-in, best dressed"-basis. So, have your application ready to be submitted as soon as you have seen the property.

The 1Form will explain what supporting documents you need, but some of the requirements for the 100-point check (see Chapter 6 for a more detailed explanation) will not yet be possible for you, such as a Medicare card.

Listed below are the essentials you must include:

1. **Passports.**

2. **Contract or letter of appointment** in Australia (because you won't have a payslip yet).

3. **Visa.**

4. Evidence of your **Australian bank account**, and if you have already transferred funds, then a copy of your balance.

5. **A covering letter** will be introducing you and your family. This should be about two paragraphs; anything longer will not be read. You could even include your reason for coming to Australia, a couple of photos of your current home to show you are house proud, and that you are looking forward to making memories in your first home in

Australia. Your covering letter can be a little more personal but still professional.

The purpose of the supporting documents is to show the agent who you are and if you will be able to pay the rent on an ongoing basis. If you don't have a job, you will need to prove that you have enough capital in your Australian bank account. If you do have a job, they will want to see that your job is permanent or for the duration of the lease and that the salary covers the rental price.

TO NEGOTIATE OR NOT TO NEGOTIATE

We all want the best deal, but you need to be realistic too. You don't have a credit rating in Australia, nor do you have any local references. However, that does not mean that you are not worthy, so don't resort to walking with your hat in hand. Australians will give you a fair go, but you need to be reasonable.

We generally don't negotiate a price, unless we can find a valid reason. Overall, we find that rental prices are usually fairly accurate. Once you have visited a few properties, you will have a benchmark of what is fair and what is not. If you arrive at an open inspection, and you are the only ones there (which is rare), then you will know that there is not much competition and you might try your luck. Most of the time, if you offer less, you just land up with a delay because the real estate agent comes back and declines the application, holds another OFI and gets a tenant willing to pay the asking price.

In short, unless the property has been on the market for a while, and there is little or no competition, we would not chance a negotiation. More often than not, though, adding a few dollars to your offer will rocket your application onto the shortlist. For as little as $20 per week, you can surpass any local application. Again though, don't do this if it is not necessary. There would have to be more than five other families interested in a property before we would suggest this to a client.

Offering six months' rent in advance is also an option. The only time this has any positive impact on your application is if you are arriving in Australia without a job. The option of paying rent upfront and providing proof of your bank account will appease the agent and landlord that you will be able to make your rental payments. However, offering rent in advance has administration issues for the agency, and yes, they can make some money on the interest earned before they hand the money over to the landlord on a monthly basis, but unless you are top-end rental, the interest they earn is not worth the effort.

WHAT MAKES YOU A STRONG APPLICANT?

This is perhaps one of the first times in Australia that you will feel like the carpet has been pulled out from under you. Nobody knows your history or understands that you are genuinely a great person. Everything is determined by what is on paper.

Relax! Despite you not having a local credit history, you will have supplied enough supporting documents because we will have prepared you well!

What you do have in your favour is that you can move in as soon as possible, you do not need to give a month's notice on your current rental. You even have flexibility if the landlord needs to do some repairs once the current tenant moves out.

Remember, you are a house-proud person and will look after the property well. Don't underestimate the power of a covering letter. Like we said, just a couple of paragraphs introducing your family, your reason for coming to Australia and how you will care for the property makes your application more personal.

Try to refer to something specific you noticed, like a particular flower or a stained-glass window, to create rapport with the landlord.

SUMMARY OF RECOMMENDATIONS

1. Identify your unique anchor.

2. Narrow down suburbs using your anchor and budget.

3. When choosing your temporary accommodation, choose convenience.

4. Make a checklist of what you want to look at in a potential rental property.

5. Prepare your rental applications in advance, including your written references.

6. Be a confident applicant, and remember: "First-in, best dressed"!

5

MOVING WITH CHILDREN

"You can't be that kid standing at the top of the waterslide,
overthinking it. You have to go down the chute."

~ *Tina Fey (American actress)*

We, as parents worry so much about our children. How will
they adapt? Will they make friends? Will they be anxious?

The answer to all of these questions is: yes! But will they
suffer? Not likely at all! The long-term positive effects far
outweigh any short-term stress.

Will they be enriched, more worldly, and have a unique
experience? Absolutely.

UNSEEN LESSONS
There are lessons and skills that children, and you, for that
matter, will learn on a subconscious level. People who have to
adapt to a new environment develop skills as a natural instinct
to survive.

Reading body language is one of those skills. Even though you are moving to a country where you will probably still speak the same language, you will become acutely aware of the body language of people in your new environment, to assess a situation.

You will become more observant because you have so much to learn and everything is new, such as signage, parking restrictions and menus. Everything around you will demand more attention from your senses and subconscious mind.

In the book *Third Culture Kids*, the authors compare children to chameleons. They observe, adjust themselves a little, observe again and readjust, all while moving slowly to blend in.

These are the unseen lessons your children will be learning. This will not only enrich their lives but will also make them more empathetic and self-aware.

Children who have moved countries make friends much more easily because of these refined interpersonal skills. Not to mention the skills they are developing for later in life.

YOUR ROLE AS PARENTS

Children live in the moment; they don't plan too far ahead. We, as parents, are worrying way too far in advance. Take it from us, all that worrying (and voicing it) only makes our children anxious.

Our stress levels are what unsettles children, and they start to build their own barriers and defences to protect themselves. If the unknown is giving you, the adult, a lot of stress, just imagine what it must do to a child.

All children, even siblings, are different and will react differently to stressors of the move. Your family values and rules should be stable and unwavering before you start the moving process, and they must remain in force during a move.

Children need boundaries, which will provide them with stability and something familiar. Their whole world will be rocked to the core, and they should be able to find comfort in the security of a strong family bond.

Be consistent and stick to the same rules that you had back home. Things like honesty, good manners, friendship and kindness provide a strong foundation.

Please be mindful that the first few weeks of your relocation, with a new job, and your child starting school will be exhausting. This is true even when your child might start school long after you have arrived in Australia.

Think for a minute how much the kids will be observing around them to "save face":
1. Eating styles around the lunch box.
2. What you have packed into the lunchbox.
3. How they greet their teachers and each other.
4. Or even something as simple as how others carry their schoolbooks.

This is before they have even opened a maths book and realised the methods, they were taught in their home country are very different from the methods in Australia. If your home language is not English, children will be ten times more tired from the information overload. Be patient with them!

One thing we would recommend to all parents is to be a good listener. Too often, in the stress of the moment, parents are forceful and excessively strict or dismissive, without listening to the concerns of their child/ren. Remember that everyone has a different perspective, and the concerns children have are genuinely worrying them.

For you, as the adult, it is a simple fix, but you will not be able to help your child/ren if you don't take the time to listen and comfort them.

When your child/ren expresses that they don't want to leave their friends behind, don't say: "Oh, but you will make new friends." That is not what they need to hear. Their friends are the world to them right now. Don't make them feel like their friends are not important, or even worse, disposable. Explain that their friends are not going anywhere, and you will know where to find them when you come back to visit.

Depending on their age, remind them that they can Skype with their friends. It is important to remind children that just because you are moving to a new country, it does not mean that everything back home will be gone forever. All you will be doing is making more friends in Australia.

If time allows, then plan a "farewell party". It is an excellent distraction for a young child/ren to have a party with all their friends. One family we moved had the fantastic idea of hiring a photo booth. It was so much fun and provided a set of photos for the hosts and the friends being left behind. This is especially a good idea for teenagers.

Real-life story

When we relocated from France to the United Kingdom (UK), my daughter took the school bag she used at her school in France on her first day to the new school in the UK. The other kids teased her about it on her first day, and she was forever known as "the girl with the suitcase".

WHEN TO TELL THE CHILDREN?

With older children, it can be quite far in advance. Teenagers don't like to be forced into anything. As much as you want to involve them in the decision-making process, this is too big a decision for them to deal with at this early stage. After interviewing a number of parents who had moved with teenagers, the general consensus was to keep opening their eyes to the possibility, long before the move is even definite.

If you think you are going to encounter resistance, then start early by dropping hints like: "Do you know that in Australia you can take Forensic Science as a school subject?" or: "Oh, wow, I see in year nine in Australia they go the Great Barrier Reef for biology camp. A week on a boat with friends!"

Don't underestimate their intelligence by dropping hints too frequently, though! If you are leaving a more hostile country, then point out differences and what you are looking forward to in Australia, obviously in line with their interests and future.

The next time you raise the subject, you could ask what they think, because no doubt they will have been brewing over the idea since you last discussed it. Take it slowly with teenagers and show them the benefits of moving to Australia. Teenagers are not interested in the same reasons you are, especially not the long-term ones. Get down to their level and use reasoning to entice them with things that interest them.

Do your homework and find out how they will benefit from the move in a direct way that is here and now. They can't and won't relate to the ten-year benefit.

You can influence their decisions, but we would not recommend saying: "It's your decision". That puts immense pressure on an already highly strung or nervous teen. Despite their mood swings, for the most part, they usually just want to make you happy. No doubt, the stubborn teenager will immediately challenge you. Always be honest and say you are investigating options because of reasons A, B and C.

It is a little easier with younger children, but you should still take their concerns seriously, as futile as you might think they are. It is not recommended to tell younger children too far in advance, especially if they have no concept of time yet. Ideally, if you can leave it until 12-18 weeks before the move, then you have done well.

When we moved internationally with small children, my husband and I never discussed anything about the move until the children had gone to bed. These adult debates can be stressful for a child. You might just be comparing job offers and various prospects, all of which could change in the next few days, but it may unsettle the children.

You do not want to be saying to any child: "Well, we might do this, and go to place XYZ, but if that can't happen, we might have to change to place ABC." Give children the facts, not wishy-washy possibilities. Instead explain to a young child that you are going to pack up all their things carefully because you found this great house near the beach in Melbourne, and there is a school with loads of slides. Then you are on the right track.

We know this is easier said than done because chances are you have not been to Australia to visit, and you haven't found the house and the school yet, but at this early stage that is okay.

Know what will entice your child and use every trick in the book to make it sound exciting. Younger children are more visual, so sit with them to show them a book on Australia and see what they like. From about four weeks before the move, you can use a calendar to mark off the days.

Let your children decorate their carton boxes. Buy a variety of stickers to assist with the creative process. Children can become very protective of their possessions during this time. They don't want the disruption, nor do they want strangers touching their toys and belongings. Tell them they can have a carton box for their "best" toys, and this is the box they can decorate. It gives them a sense of relief and understanding that those toys are going to be okay.

Don't worry about how it is packed or if they only put three things in the carton box; just let them be comfortable with what they are doing. You may even need to make some holes in the top of the carton box because "Teddy" is scared of the dark. That is fine, make the holes! You want to make sure the child is relaxed, and there is a sense of fun for them.

We can assure you, the look on their faces when their own decorated carton box arrives in Australia, is priceless.

A child's sense of smell is also very acute, and you can use this to your advantage. Introduce a relaxing scent around your home before you leave, which you can replicate in Australia. This will create a sense of familiarity.

Scents such as chamomile, lavender, jasmine and basil are all relaxing and will bring a level of comfort to your child in their new or changing surroundings.

THE AUSTRALIAN SCHOOL SYSTEM

The school system in Australia is recognised around the world as being of a very high standard, and some of the Australian universities sit in the top 2% of the world. With this knowledge, you can feel confident that choosing a school here is easy. Depending on your motivation and budget, you have some choices:

- State school
- Semiprivate school
- Private school
- All girls
- All boys
- Parallel education

All children must be in school by their sixth birthday. Most children will start prep from the age of five years. As with most things in Australia, the starting age can vary from state to state.

The schools in Australia do focus on the social development of children, so even if you have a child that excels at school, they believe in children being with those of their own age.

We do know of occasions when this has been reassessed once the child has started school, but usually, they will commence with children of the same age. Generally, the class sizes are around 23 to a maximum of 27 students.

School is compulsory until the age of 16 years. At the end of year 12, children will attain a certificate similar to a Senior Certificate. The name of this certificate varies amongst the states.

In most instances, children obtain an ATAR (Australian Tertiary Admission Rank) score, which is a score they will need for enrolment for university courses. There are different score requirements, depending on the choice of the course, being studied. Further education in Australia includes university or Vocational Education and Training (VET) – which can be compared to Technical Colleges in other countries. VET courses are delivered by TAFE colleges, so in order to do a VET subject or course, you will need to search for a TAFE college. Examples would be plumbing, hairdressing, childcare, carpentry.

School structures

There are some significant differences between state and private schools. Generally speaking, in the **state school system**, the following is applicable:

1. Primary school for year 1 to year 6 (12 years old).
2. High school (secondary school) for year 7 to year 12.

Private and semiprivate schools do it a little differently:

1. Prep or pre-school is often referred to as Early Learning Centres (ELC).
2. Year 1 to year 4 is junior school.
3. Year 5 to year 8 is middle school.
4. Year 9 is pre-senior school.
5. Year 10 to year 12 is senior school.

These schools tend to all be at the same campus so you can remain in the area for the entire time your child is at school.

School glossary

There are a variety of names across the states that refer to schools, and even the structure within the schools can vary across states and the nation. To help you with further research, it is important that you have a reference; otherwise, it all becomes very confusing:

1. **Government schools** may also be called "state" or "public" schools.

2. **Private schools** may also be called "independent" schools.

3. **Pre-schools** may also be called "ELC", "pre-prep", "prep" or "kindergarten".

4. **Primary school** may also be called "junior college" or "junior school".

5. **High school** may also be called "secondary" school, "senior" school or "senior" college.

6. **Tertiary education** is "higher education", anything you

choose after school – University or Technical and Further Education (TAFE).

School curriculum
The school curriculum covers seven key learning areas, namely:
1. English
2. Mathematics
3. Sciences
4. Technology
5. Arts
6. Health and physical education
7. LOTE (languages other than English)

In Australia, there are 80 subjects that are considered for year 12 (final year). That does not mean every school teaches all 80 subjects, though. If you are considering a high school, you may want to investigate the subjects they offer as part of your shortlisting process.

CHOICE OF SCHOOL
If you have not already read the section on budgeting for schooling, then best you read it first. Your budget will be the driving force behind deciding on schooling because the difference in cost is staggering.

Most government schools are free, whereas private or semiprivate schools are not! You should also know that depending on your visa, and which state you will be living in, even the government schools might not be free.

For example, if you are on a temporary working visa (such as a 457 skills visa) and thinking of living in Sydney (State of New South Wales), then you will pay school fees even at government schools.

In New South Wales your children are considered as international students and fees can be as high as those for a private school. This is a no brainer because the private schools offer more opportunities for your child.

In the State of Victoria, this is not the case for around 90%

of government schools, where government schools are still free for temporary work visa holders.

We encourage you to check the respective website for your proposed state or territory. Search online by typing: Department of Education Victoria (or South Australia or New South Wales, etc.).

It is not unusual in Australia to send children to state primary schools but private high schools. If your budget allows it, then try to consider this option. The state high schools are good, but there are fewer of them spread out over a wider catchment zone. This may not only cause problems with finding housing in the catchment zone, but what if you have a child in each – primary and high school? You are better off focusing on the primary school zone and using a private high school (not zoned).

Schooling is one of the strong "anchors" we discussed in Chapter 3. Because you will most likely "do the school run" every day, it should take careful consideration to keep your life simple. Think about parties, sport and playdates. Your new life will centre around schools whether you like it or not.

State schools

State schools have an obligation to enrol your child if your home is within their catchment zone. You, therefore, don't need to contact them early. Most school websites have a map of their catchment area on their website under the "Enrolment" section.

If a school is your deciding factor or anchor in the search for a rental property, print out its zone map and keep referring to it during your home search.

State schools do not have marketing departments or employees dedicated to the enrolment process. Don't expect them to roll out a red carpet and bow to your list of questions from where you are currently in the world.

You may get a really cold reception but don't let this put you off. The administrative department is often under-resourced and very busy. An email from a prospective family who is not in the country and who might not even live in their school zone will just go to the bottom of the pile. Be assured though that they are working hard at looking after the children already in their care. State schools don't owe you anything, but they are there if you need them.

You should be aware that some areas do have enrolment "caps" in place, but this is relatively rare. This happens when an area has grown quickly, and the school doesn't have enough resources to cope with the sudden growth. In this case, you may be referred to the next closest school.

For primary schools, this is not too much of a problem, because there is an abundance of primary schools, and you might only be referred to a school a short distance away.

For high schools, this could be an issue. High schools are further apart from each other. If you are directed to another high school, it might not be as convenient.

As we mentioned already, though, remember that teenagers have access to the excellent public transportation system, and they needn't be driven everywhere. It is "so uncool" to be driven to school anyway!

Private and semiprivate schools

Let's start off with some background concerning semiprivate schools. They are, generally speaking, faith-based schools. In the good old days, the faith-based schools received contributions from the affiliated churches.

Today those contributions come from the government. Hence, semiprivate schools cost around half the price of private schools.

However, you will need to provide proof that you are "practising" a particular religion. We have found that some of the schools are not quite as particular, though. They are just happy to get more "bums on seats".

A written reference letter from your church leader and any baptism certificate or similar paperwork will support your application.

Parents could also be invited to attend an informal

interview with the school principal and other selected trustee or board members.

A word of caution:

If you are enrolling children into state or semiprivate schools in the middle of the school year, you might encounter some resistance. In order to gain their government contributions, schools claim from the government based on their headcount at the end of April each year. If you are trying to enrol a child from the second term, the school will have to carry the cost of your child without any government rebate. We only really come across this problem for the second and third term, because by the time it gets to the fourth term, the school has the commitment of your enrolment for the following year, so they are more accommodating.

Private schools and semiprivate schools are far more accommodating regarding your queries from where you are currently residing. Feel free to contact these schools early and check on spaces. They have dedicated enrolment officers – thus you will have enrolment fees to pay! Private schools are not zoned, which means that you can enrol your children prior to finding your home. This can be a real bonus in your relocation process. Ask the school if they offer any school buses and if so, if they can send you the bus routes. This can help to extend your rental search area.

Top tip: *If you are choosing a school based on bus routes, be sure to check bus seat availability. It is not good to consider this option if there are no available seats on the buses. The enrolment officer might not share that information with you early on.*

Further reading and websites we recommend:
1. **Private schools** (www.privateschoolsdirectory.com.au).
2. **Australian Association of Christian Schools** (www.aacs.net.au).
3. **The Australian Schools Directory** (www.australianschoolsdirectory.com.au). On this website

you can also search for specialised schools like Montessori, Steiner, Performing Arts and special needs schools.

SHORTLISTING SCHOOLS

You can start doing your homework while you are still in your home country and narrow down your school search, but you need to know what you are looking for and how to compare the schools.

It is important that your research is based on the state you will be living in. There are differences between the states in the way schools operate.

Any school is only as good as its teachers, and you need to find a school that will suit your child.

Here are some considerations:

1. **School population:** Will a big school or smaller school be best for your child?

2. **LOTE** – Languages other than English. Schools here offer a wide range of Asian and European languages. Do you have a preference, either by continent or language? Please note that Afrikaans is not a school subject in Australia.

3. **Sport, clubs, and activities.**

4. **Teaching methods:** Montessori, Steiner or International Baccalaureate?

5. For **high school children**, which school offers the subjects your child requires for his or her future studies?

6. **Suburb or area**, if you know this already.

School ranking websites

Before you look at the individual school websites, there are a couple of websites where you can quickly assess schools by area, population and ranking. Most people like to start with the school's ranking.

We are not convinced that these ranking websites are comparing apples with apples, though. Take the rankings with a pinch of salt. It may be helpful to look at specific trends, such as if the school has improved over the years.

A good place to start is the **Better Education** website. This website is not a favourite, but you can at least get a sense of where the schools are ranked. This website only uses Maths and English, and you can sort the lists by state and other relevant categories: www.bettereducation.com.au

Perhaps a more concise website for gathering information, seeing trends and equal comparison, is the (somewhat controversial) website **My School.**

It is controversial because, when the website was launched in 2012, there were many schools that were not happy with the information that was available to the public.

A few schools took the opportunity to use the My School website as another marketing platform, and they prepared their students for weeks to ensure they had the best NAPLAN (see next paragraph) test results. We encourage you to use this website as a guide only. It is a very subjective source of information and may not paint as clear a picture as you might think.

What we do like about this website is that you can see the school population, teacher ratios, balance of students by girl/boy, ethnic background, how many go on to further education, etc. It has many facts in an easy and user-friendly format to compare with other schools: www.myschool.edu.au

The My School-website results are based on **NAPLAN** results. NAPLAN (National Assessment Program) tests are written tests conducted every year across Australia.

They are usually taken around early May. Every child, regardless of state or private schooling, will write the exact same test on the same day.

NAPLAN tests assess English and Maths levels and are meant as a guide to ensure that the Australian National Curriculum is meeting the needs of children and that there is progress across the country. Every learner in year 3, 5, 7 and 9 writes these tests.

You can find out more about NAPLAN here: www.nap.edu.au

School website marketing

Now is a good time to move on to the school website. Arm yourself with your checklist of what you want from a school and the information and patterns you may have gained from the Better Education and My School websites.

Perhaps a few questions on your checklist have not yet been answered. The specific school website could provide further information. This could concern the LOTE (Languages other than English) or the sports programs, after school care, the catchment zone and the recent newsletters.

Keep in mind that a school website is a marketing tool, so here are some tips on assessing a school from its website:

The principal's message:
This section will provide valuable information on the values. Do they align with your values?
Is this the key message and values you want to be conveyed to your child?

School newsletters:
Does the school deliver what it promises on the website?
The school newsletter will give you a glimpse of sport accolades, social issues and the school culture, without the marketing hype on the website.

Parental portal:
Many schools now have these portals on their websites which you can only access once your child is enrolled at the school. However, this is a good time to see if it is offered on the school website to indicate their advancement in IT and if there will be clear communication with the parents.

Many migrants will already be familiar with such portals where parents can monitor reports, write private emails to teachers, access book lists and order lunch.

CHILDREN'S SCHOOLING NEEDS

Immunisation schedule (NIP schedule)

Children whose National Immunisation Program (NIP) schedule (www.health.gov.au/health-topics/immunisation) is not up to date are not allowed to attend school, family day-care or other community activities or be transported in an ambulance. Under the current COVID-19 pandemic regulations, the rules on immunisation have tightened. Before a child can commence school, they need to produce a certificate from the Australian Immunisation Register (AIR). This certificate can take anything from two to six weeks to obtain in some areas. Attend to your child's immunisation sooner rather than later so that you can receive the certificate in time for them to commence school. For more information visit: www.servicesaustralia.gov.au/individuals/services/medicare/australian-immunisation-register

School uniforms and shoes

Australians all wear a school uniform, and most will wear black (or brown) leather shoes, so don't get rid of the school shoes.

School lunches

School lunches are not provided. Children will need a mid-morning snack, and lunch and younger children will often have another snack break. In an attempt to eliminate plastic in lunch boxes, the "naked food" concept was introduced. Leave the sandwich unwrapped or "naked".

Most schools will have a canteen (tuckshop), where children can buy lunch too. The canteen is usually run by an outside company, not the school itself, so there is usually a good selection of healthy and junk food.

For junior school, there is usually an Eski (cooler box) in

the classroom. The class leaders take the Eski to the canteen, where it is filled with individual orders. This way, young children are not handling money or standing in the lunch queue, and the teacher can monitor them while eating.

Sun protection
Children should also have sunscreen and bottled water with them. During summer a school hat is compulsory.

Food allergies
You should be acutely aware of the no nuts policy. Just don't put nuts in the lunchbox – no peanut butter, no trail mix, no nuts whatsoever! Schools are very strict in this regard, as they will be held responsible if a child should suffer an anaphylactic reaction. The same should be said if you are sending any party bags or cake to the class for your child's birthday. Always check with the teacher before you send anything. Be prepared to provide a list of all the ingredients with the food items.

If you are the parent of an anaphylactic child, be assured that the schools know how to handle this. Most children will be required to provide two EpiPens to be kept at school. One is for the school nurse and the other for the child's school bag. You must go to your general practitioner (GP) and obtain a prescription for your EpiPen. Without a prescription, you will pay around $120 per EpiPen and with a script, around $30.

The schools will have an anaphylactic action plan for each child, and this action plan is signed off by your GP in order to obtain a script at the same time.

Books and stationery
In primary school just about all books and stationery are supplied by the school. As part of the school uniform, you will need also to buy a "book bag" which is for their nightly reading book and library books.

At the high school, you will receive a book and stationery list, which is usually ordered online and delivered to the school before the start of the new school year. You can pay a fee to have the heavy carton box delivered to your home, and you can take it to school yourself. The only time children might do this, is to have their books ahead of the school year, if they want to start studying (said no child ever!) or wrap them in plastic.

Most schools will have a second-hand bookstore, or sometimes a Facebook page, where you can buy books from previous students. Just make sure that you are buying the correct edition of the book.

Top tip: *Don't leave it until the last minute. You will have to fight the crowds in the shops and do it yourself. We generally find children prefer their own stationery rather than the "bulk standard" from the online bookstore.*

Bring Your Own Device (BYOD)
In some schools, pupils must bring their own laptop (specifications will be supplied by the school). Of course, the school may insist on an iPad. Some schools will supply the device, and the cost will be included in your school fees.

SPORT AND CLUBS
It is not unusual for pupils to finish their school day and make their way, in a group, to the local sports grounds. The senior children will often mentor and coach the younger groups, with only a few parents involved.

Sport during school hours
Generally speaking, there is very little sport conducted within the state/government primary schools, apart from swimming and athletics. Unless there is a teacher at the school who is passionate about a sport and he or she offers to host a program in soccer, footy (Australian football) or netball, it won't happen.

Think of your state school as a community school. The children go to the local school and belong to the local sports club. Very often the local sports club will use the school ovals, but the sports events/practice are not conducted within the school program.

The children will still participate in Physical Education (PE), but there is often not a school team for soccer or netball until they get to high school. Obviously, there are still competitions between the states for each sport, so your child may get the opportunity to represent his or her school in a state or national team.

Let's take cricket, for example. The school might not have a cricket team, but every year, when the state schools sports body is putting together a state school team, your children can go to the trials to represent their school and hopefully their state. You can read more here and see the diversity of sports children can enjoy: www.schoolsportaustralia.edu.au

Private schools have facilities within the school grounds to offer a wider range of sports. It is the Australian way for everyone to "give it a go" and to have "a fair go". Learners are rotated around different sports to find their best fit and expose them to as many sports as possible. Saturday sport is usually compulsory in private schools.

In primary schools, learners might have a choice between three to four sports from which to choose one for the term. In high school they tend to have a winter and summer sport. Once again, there are choices depending on the school, and they can choose between four and seven sports.

Most private schools will have serious interschool competitions, with rival schools attracting quite a crowd! Private schools mostly follow the APS-track and will compete against other private schools.

There are groups and teams for just about any sport activity, with clear development pathways for all sports. For more examples, visit the following websites:

www.milo.com.au/sports
www.netsetgo.asn.au
www.hotshots.tennis.com.au

Learn2Swim

Australia has a very well-developed program for swimming. In 2016, 280 people drowned in open water, rivers and swimming pools in Australia. Since then, there has been an urgency to teach everyone to swim. Toddlers were a large percentage of the drownings, and for that reason, the Learn2Swim-program was introduced. It commences with free lessons at a number of locations in October. You can find out more about this program at www.kidsalive.com.au

Elite sport

We could not possibly cover every sport here, but if your child is already at an elite sports level, there are many "sports" schools or academies. A huge amount of government funding goes towards increasing sport participation within state schools, and more and more schools are offering better sports facilities.

We would suggest you search online by sport type and the state in which you will settle. These schools have dedicated coaches, and learners will spend part of their day being coached in their particular sport.

Usually, learners do not study a second language and do not participate in normal PE classes. Instead, this time in the curriculum is taken up by their chosen sport with dedicated, qualified coaches.

An example would be Rowville Sports Academy near Melbourne:
www.rowvillesc.vic.edu.au/rowville-sports-academy-2/

AFTER SCHOOL CARE

Most schools offer before and after school care, which is run by an outside company called **Camp Australia**. Camp Australia will use the school hall or library to host the children, and in most circumstances, the care will include a snack, if the facilities allow for it. The hours of care may vary, please read more here: www.campaustralia.com.au

INTERNATIONAL BACCALAUREATE

Yes, there are schools offering the International Baccalaureate. At the moment, a total of 130 primary schools and 73 high schools are offering the diploma across Australia – that is out of around 9 000 schools!

Choosing the IB-program will depend on your circumstances, but the general consensus is that the level of education in the Australian curriculum is of a high standard and is widely accepted in universities around the world.

The International Baccalaureate in primary school is of little importance. Unless, of course, you are an ex-pat family who will be moving internationally, a number of times, and you are looking for continuity in your child's curriculum.

CHILDREN AND THE SOCIAL SCENE

Younger children

Whether a party is hosted at your home or a venue depends on your personal preference. Parties outside the home might be a swimming party, an indoor inflatable park or an animal petting zoo. The list is endless. It is not unusual to just meet in the local park where the host will supply picnic food.

Generally, parties at home will include some sort of entertainment, maybe face painting, balloon sculpting or something similar.

Food is always provided, as well as a party bag to take home.

Gifts are welcome. Usually, the presents are placed on a table to be opened after the party. Upon arrival, your child should find the birthday child and hand him or her the present, unless you are directed to the gift table.

Generally, up to the age of around seven years old, parents remain at the party venue for the duration of the party.

Teenagers and older children

For older children, there are two types of parties in Australia: a "party" or a "gath". A gath is a small gathering of people, usually around 10-35 people, having a BBQ or just pizza. A party is a traditional party with music and dancing. Of course, this doesn't mean that a gath won't have blaring music!

Children and alcohol

The legal drinking age is 18, although children from the age of 16 are allowed to drink with parental consent.

There are hefty penalties for both the parent of the child and the parent, or whoever served alcohol when caught. For example, if a pub serves alcohol to an underage person, the pub may be fined anything between $1 000 and $14 000.

If you are hosting a party, you are responsible for the children in your care, and each child under 18, must supply a letter of consent from the parents. If you are the host and there are underage children, you will be fined for serving them if they do not have a note from their parents.

Uber and transport

Random Breath Tests (RBT) are frequent and hold serious fines for driving under the influence of alcohol or drugs. Under the age of 21 years, young adults must have a zero-blood alcohol level when tested.

Remember that in most states, teens are driving from the age of 17 years. For this reason, it is not unusual for them to sleepover at a party, have a designated driver or sleep at someone's house nearby in a group.

Muck-up day and schoolies

We all remember having fun on our last day of secondary school, with spray cans of shaving cream, having good, clean fun! For the most part, muck-up day is just that, and this tradition is alive and well in Australia.

Most year 12 students will dress up for the occasion, in fact, they will stay in those clothes all day, regardless of what they might do or celebrate after school. There is usually some prank played on a teacher or two. Water guns are common.

Of course, there are those children who can spoil it for

everyone. That is why some schools are banning the day or bringing in security to maintain peace. All in all, it is usually just good fun!

"Schoolies" is every parent's nightmare unless you are Australian and "get it". This is a week-long end of school festival held at a few key locations around Australia. There have been reports of young ones getting into fights, being drunk in public or overdosing on drugs.

Over the years, security at these events has become very strict. The area is well patrolled, with a selection of hotels and streets closed off for the event.

Bookings are made via the school website on a schoolies portal. You can find out more here: www.schoolies.com

Real-life story

For our peace of mind as parents, we gave our daughter two options at the end of year 12 – a holiday of her choice or schoolies with her friends. She could take a friend with if she chose the holiday.

She decided on a cruise vacation to New Zealand to visit all the Lord of The Rings movie locations like the Shire, Hobbiton, the Weta Studios in Wellington and Fiordland. We all thoroughly enjoyed the vacation, and she had no regrets about missing out on schoolies week.

SETTLING CHILDREN IN AUSTRALIA

We have mentioned how family rules should remain consistent. This is the base and grounding for your move, so make sure everyone knows the house rules.

One of the reasons for this is that everybody deals with the stress of a relocation differently. Know your child and make sure the communication lines are open, but also be aware of how stress manifests inside of them.

Girls tend to get emotional while boys tend to display anger and take it out on you for something very mundane. Recognise these traits in your child, so that later on, when you are all a little frayed and Johnny is upset about the flavour of the cheese, know that it has actually nothing to do with the cheese.

Yes, family values and rules are especially important, but when it comes to teenagers, you need to be a little more flexible. Sometimes, and within reason, you need to "pick your battles". In the first few weeks, allow a little freedom, but remind them of the rules. For example, if there is a family rule of "finishing all your food" but Johnny is tired and irritable, you should remind him of the rule, but say that you will let it go this time because you understand that it has been a long day.

You get the idea? Reinforce the rule but also show respect for your child's feelings. Be in touch with her emotions; try to understand and be a good listener.

One of the first loves for Australians is the love of sport, so even if you are not a sporting family, you should know that sport is discussed, analysed, dissected, and compared.

Imagine for a minute you arrived in England, for example, and did not know what a soccer ball looked like or how the game worked. The same can be said for your child arriving on the school playground in Australia. It is important to have some basic knowledge of sport here in Australia.

Make every effort to get involved and help your children feel included in the playground banter.

Top tip: *After about three months in Australia, plan a long weekend or a week away, if it is possible. You need to regroup after a move and just relax around each other again. It is important, and we really wish everybody would consider this.*

SUMMARY OF RECOMMENDATIONS

1. Use this summary to assist you in finding the best school:
    *   Make a list of what is important to you and your child in a school.
    *   Decide if you are considering state, semiprivate or private schooling.
    *   Use the school rankings and NAPLAN results to shortlist.
    *   Check the school website to include or eliminate a school.
    *   If you are considering a private or semiprivate school, feel free to contact the school.
    *   If you are considering a government school, then familiarize yourself with its catchment zone – and start narrowing down your home search area.

2. Be a good listener. If you aren't a good listener, now is the right time to start improving those listening skills. Pick your battles and understand that everybody has a different perspective on what is important to him or her.

3. Regroup as a family; plan a short getaway around 3-6 months after arriving.

6

EVERYDAY AUSTRALIAN LIFE

"What is the difference between Australia and yoghurt?
Yoghurt has more culture!"

~ Allan and Barbara Pease
(Aussie joke from their book, The Answer)

Everyday life in Australia is something we could never have imagined, and yet it is so uncomplicated and straightforward. The point is that in Australia you can just get on with life, *your* life.

In this chapter, we want to make you see how straightforward things can be. When we help migrants relocate, they are always expecting it to be an "absolute nightmare" to change their driver's licence, connect utilities or get a Medicare card. We often find that migrants arrive here with such a sense of anxiety, which is not at all needed.

It is a process, and there is a specific way to do everything in a timely fashion, but it is all straightforward.

BUSINESS HOURS

The standard number of working hours in Australia is 38 hours per week. Most business hours are from 9am to 5:30pm. Shopping centres tend to have the same hours, however on Thursday and Friday evenings; hours are usually extended to around 9pm.

Furniture retailers, however, might open as late as 10am. In some areas, grocery stores are open 24 hours or may only close at midnight and reopen again at 6am.

State schools are generally open from 9am to 3pm or 3:30pm.

AUSTRALIAN PUBLIC HOLIDAYS

Public holiday dates for Labour Day and the Queen's Birthday vary from state to state. When a public holiday falls on a Saturday or Sunday, the following Monday is observed.

- New Year's Day (1 January)
- Australia Day (26 January)
- Labour Day (1st Monday in March)
- Easter, Good Friday, and Easter Monday (April)
- Anzac Day (25 April)
- Reconciliation Day (27 May)
- Queen's Birthday (2nd Monday in June)
- Labour Day (7 October)
- Christmas (25 December)
- Boxing Day (26 December)

Victoria only public holidays

- AFL Grand Final (28 September)
- Melbourne Cup (1st Tuesday in November)

AUSTRALIAN TIME ZONES

Australia has three time zones:
1. Eastern Standard Time (EST)
2. Central Standard Time (CST)
3. Western Standard Time (WST)

State	Standard Time	Daylight Saving Time
Western Australia	+8 hours GMT	No change
Northern Territory	+9.5 hours GMT	No change
South Australia	+9.5 hours GMT	10.5 hours GMT
Queensland	+10 hours GMT	No change
New South Wales & ACT	+10 hours GMT	+11 hours GMT
Victoria (Melbourne)	+10 hours GMT	+11 hours GMT
Tasmania	+10 hours GMT	+11 hours GMT

DAYLIGHT SAVING TIME

Australia introduced daylight saving time (DST) in various forms since the early 1900s. While the majority of Australians accept it, daylight savings has been rejected repeatedly by others. Western Australians voted in 2009 and for the fourth time it was rejected.

Arguments for and against daylight savings often become heated as people are passionate on both sides. Queensland has been considering splitting the state in half with only one part participating in daylight saving.

ACT • Victoria • Tasmania • New South Wales • South Australia (participate in daylight savings)

From 2008, the ACT, NSW, South Australia, Victoria and Tasmania all implemented daylight savings from the first Sunday in October, ending on the first Sunday in April. This now results in an extra month of daylight savings for the ACT. More importantly, it introduces a standard start and finish date in these states.

Daylight savings begins on the first Sunday in October, with clocks being set forward one hour at 2am.

Daylight savings ends on the first Sunday in April, with clocks being set back one hour at 2am.

Queensland • Northern Territory • Western Australia (do not participate in daylight savings)

ROSTERED DAYS OFF (RDO'S)

In the 1980s when a 38-hour working week was introduced, it meant that the average working day would be seven hours and 36 minutes. For shift workers, this became an issue, so it was decided (mostly by unions) that work agreements could be compiled in 152 work hour cycles, not exceeding 28 days. This allowed for 19 working days of eight hours each, with the 20th day rostered off. RDO's can run on different cycles for each industry, but regardless of this, it really eases traffic congestion on RDO days!

FINANCIAL YEAR AND TAXES

The Australian financial year commences on 1 July and ends on 30 June. Self-completed individual tax returns are due by 31 October. Should you use a registered tax agent, you will be advised of your lodgement due date, but generally, it is by 31 March of the following year.

We recommend that you use a registered tax agent when you arrive in Australia. Newly arrived immigrants don't know what tax-deductible is and what isn't, and professional advice is valuable.

The tax agents' fee can be deducted from the next year's tax. It is usually not hard to find a tax agent in Australia, who is familiar with your obligations for tax back in your home country if you still have investments there.

YOUR 100-POINT IDENTIFICATION CHECK

When you arrive, you will be asked to provide documentation for a 100-point check. The points system applies to people opening new financial accounts across Australia, such as a bank account, rental application, and a driver's licence.

Points are allocated to the types of documentary proof of identity that the person can produce, and you must have at least 100 points of identification to be able to establish the account. One of the first times you will be asked for your 100-point check, is on your rental application.

Most of the documents required for this check will not be available to you within the first few weeks of arrival. This is the list of documents we normally provide to the real estate agent when relocating an international arrival:

1. **Passport.**

2. **Employee contract or letter of offer** (document that states your salary, start date and that the job is full time). You can also ask your new HR department to provide a letter with a company letterhead to this effect.

3. **A screenshot or copy of your Australian bank account**, showing your balance. This is a good idea if you have deposited your moving expenses into the account.

These three documents will prove to the real estate agent that you have a job that will cover the rent and that you have enough investments in Australia.

Documents and relevant point allocation
Some institutions have their own points system, but these are generally the requirements:

1. **Primary documents**
   Only one of these permitted (70 points):
   - Passport
   - Birth certificate
   - Citizenship certificate

2. **Secondary documents**
   To make up the remaining 30 points, you may only use one document from each of the below categories:

   Document must have a photograph and name (40 points):
   - Australian driver's licence
   - Working with children check
   - Social security card
   - Tertiary education student ID card

<u>Document must have a name and address (35 points):</u>
- Utility bill, e.g. electricity, gas, or telephone
- Bank statement
- Council rates notice
- Lease/rental agreement
- Motor vehicle registration or insurance documents

<u>Document must have a name and signature (25 points):</u>
- Credit or debit card
- Foreign driver's licence
- Medicare card
- Marriage certificate (for maiden name only)

HOUSEHOLD WASTE AND RECYCLING

You should check your local council website for specific information and regulations that are relevant to your council area. Many councils will send you a "New home pack" if you request it on their website.

Generally, you are provided with the following three bins:

1. **Household waste** – general rubbish.

2. **Recycling** – plastic, tins, bottles, paper, and cardboard.

3. **Garden refuse** – grass cuttings, small branches.

Each local council area has different colour lids to indicate what rubbish goes in which bin, so check with your local council. The Which bin website has a great alphabetical list: www.whichbin.sa.gov.au/a-z-items
Leave your bin on the edge of the pavement, with the lid opening towards the road. If you're unsure, just check what the neighbours are doing.

Most local councils arrange a free annual hard rubbish collection. They will collect items such as scrap iron, furniture, household appliances and timber. You will receive a flyer in the mailbox which will explain what you can place out and the date on which it will be collected.

Please note: *It is illegal and considered theft to remove anything from someone's pavement. A knock on the front door is more polite. In saying this, we have never known someone to call the police to report "curb shopping." Other local councils have a booking system. You book and pay for the hard rubbish collection in advance and receive a big label through the mail. When you put the rubbish out on the nature strip, the label must be fixed to the rubbish in clear view.*

CONVERSION CHARTS

Please note that these are approximate guides only, clothing can vary according to the manufacturer's specifications. It is a good idea to familiarise yourself with your size in either European or American sizes, which is easier to convert to Australian sizes.

Many shops, both online and instore, will have size charts that convert European or American to Australian sizes. It can sometimes be a challenge to find a shop where the staff knows your country-specific sizes.

Ladies' Top/Dress Sizes

Australia	6	8-10	12-14	16	18	20	22
American	2	4	6	8	10	12	14
Europe	32	34	36	38	40	42	44
Japan	5	7	9	11	13	15	17

Men's Trouser Sizes

Australia	6	8	10	12	14	16	18
American (inches)	28	30	32	34	36	38	40
Europe	42	44	46	48	50	52	54

Men's Shirt Sizes

Australia	6	8-10	12-14	16	18	20	22
American	14	14.5	15	15.5	16	16.5	17
Europe	36	37	38	39	40	42	44
Japan	87	91	97	102	107	112	117

Ladies' Shoe Sizes

Australia	5	6	7	8	9	10	11
American	5.5	5.5	6	6	7	8	9
Europe	36	37	38	39	40	41	42
Japan	22	22.5	23	23.5	24	24.5	25

Men's Shoe Sizes

Australia	4	5	6	7	8	9	10
American	6	6	7	7	8	9	10
Europe	37	38	39	40	41	42	43
Japan	25	25.5	26	26.5	27	27.5	28

Check your current mattress size to make sure it aligns with the Australian sizes; otherwise, you may have difficulties in finding linen in Australia.

Single: 92 cm x 188 cm	**Double:** 138 cm x 188 cm
Single extra-long: 92 cm x 203 cm	**Queen:** 153 cm x 203 cm
King single: 107 cm x 203 cm	**King:** 183 cm x 203 cm

MOBILE PHONES AND INTERNET PROVIDERS

As with any first world country, there are an endless supply of mobile phone (cell phone) service providers. If you are going to use your handset from your home country, just make sure it is not blocked.

When you first arrive, you are unlikely to be able to sign up for a phone contract because you will not have sufficient supporting documents and a home address.

Therefore, it is best to use a "Pay as you go" service for the time being. We would recommend you walk into your nearest grocery store, such as Coles or Woolworths, and ask for a SIM card at the information counter. They are usually around $2. You can add credit at the counter – start with about $30 and top up as needed.

With all shopping advice in this book, we have tried to give you a range of services based on "cheap and cheerful" and "higher end." With mobile phone service providers, it works the same. We once again encourage you to shop around upon your arrival, because there is always a sale or special offer in this industry.

For a quick reference, consult websites such as www.canstar.com.au or www.youcompare.com.au

There are around 25 service providers, but here is a brief overview of the service providers we would recommend:

Major brands
- Vodafone
- Optus
- Telstra

Grocery store brands
- Coles Mobile
- ALDI Mobile
- Woolworths Mobile

Cheap and cheerful brands
- Boost Mobile
- Amaysim (Great for teenagers, when the data is finished, no automatic renewal)
- TPG
- Kogan
- LycaMobile
- Lebara
- Dodo Mobile

When you are connected to your home internet, there are often good deals you can get by purchasing a "bundle", where you can add your mobile phone, home phone, internet and digital TV into one package. Service providers such as Vodafone, Optus, Telstra and TPG offer great bundle packages.

POST AND MAIL SERVICE

Australia Post provides a domestic and international mail service. Your mail will be delivered on weekdays only. A standard letter within Australia costs $1. You can purchase individual stamps or booklets of ten stamps.

Prices for overseas mail/airmail services start at $2. There are many postal services to choose from, like bulk mail, express post with next day delivery, courier services and tracking post.

Post offices are also useful for paying bills and for buying stationery and phone cards. If you move to a new house you can have your mail redirected to the new address; you can arrange for your mail to be held while you are on holiday, or you can send international mail and packages. You will need to complete the necessary paperwork to activate this service.

You can hire a post box at the post office. Australia Post website is comprehensive, and you can search online to find your nearest shop, to search for a postcode or to calculate postage rates.

The standard red post boxes, to post your letters can be found everywhere, especially near shopping precincts. The yellow post boxes for express post services are generally only located near post offices or in large business areas.

It is worth mentioning that your mail IS delivered by the post person, so do check your mailbox at home.

For further information visit: www.auspost.com.au

Top tip: *Did you know it is a Federal Offence to dispose of someone else's mail? If you are receiving mail not addressed to you, please write "Return to Sender" on the envelope and post it in the red Post Office letterboxes.*

BANKING

We strongly recommend opening a bank account online, either before you arrive or shortly thereafter. You can, of course, walk into any bank and open an account. More often than not, you will be asked to set up an appointment, which basically means you will come back, and they will have lined up a person from every department to meet you. This is especially true for insurance, which, at this early stage, is not a priority for you.

You can open an account online up to 28 days before your arrival. You can deposit money into that account, but you won't be able to withdraw anything until after you have presented yourself in the bank with proof of identification.

Although the websites will tell you to visit a specific branch (usually their main city branch), you can, in fact, walk into any branch with your identification and account details.

New arrivals in Australia do not always speak English as a first language, and the larger city branches have employees who speak several languages. But if you can speak English, feel free to approach any of the branches.

There are four major banks in Australia, all of which offer similar services, and each will satisfy your needs upon arrival. Once you are more established and need a home loan or other services, you can change banks or do what is necessary. Don't overthink this too much; just tick it off the checklist.

The four major banks:
1. Westpac
2. NAB
3. Commonwealth
4. ANZ

Main types of transaction accounts:

1. **Cheque account:** Cheques are very rarely used. This is typically an "everyday" account.

2. **Savings account:** Can also be used as an "everyday" account, but you can't set up direct debits and such on this account.

3. **Term deposits:** A savings account with a higher interest, for long-term deposits.

4. **Credit cards:** Banks are very eager to hand these out, with

their high annual fees, transaction fees and just about anything else. Try to avoid them at all costs. Many families in Australia use a credit card so they can accumulate flight miles and other rewards, but the credit card is paid off in full every month, then reused.

If you have time and do want to do some research, we recommend **Canstar** for an overview of banking, services, offers and interest rates: www.canstar.com.au

PAYING FOR GOODS AND SERVICES

Eftpos
Electronic Funds Transfer Point of Sale (EFTPOS) is most widely used for payment in shops. Your bank will issue you with a debit card, which you can use to pay for goods and services. Remember, this is not a credit card; it is a live transfer of funds out of your account and will only work if you have money in your account; otherwise, it will be declined.

There are around 5 billion Eftpos-transactions every day across Australia. It is safe and carries little risk. Nowadays, the need for an actual Eftpos-card is declining as many people use Eftpos from their phones.

In restaurants, you may be presented with an Eftpos screen on an iPad or similar point of sale device. You can "pay pass" or "tap n go" up to $100 without inserting your pin, but transactions over $100 will require your secret pin.

Direct debit
Just like in most other countries, you can set up direct debits on your account to deduct automatically. To pay something via direct debit, you will need:
1. the name of the account,
2. the bank name,
3. your account number, and
4. the branch code (BSB).

BPay

Most companies ask for payment via BPay. Around 50 000 companies are registered for BPay. You will be provided with a BPay reference as well as a unique customer number or code. All utility bills, for example, are paid via BPay. If you see the BPay logo on an invoice or bill, look for the required information next to it.

Using your internet banking, choose "Pay a bill" and then select "BPay." Enter the BPay number, and your bank will look up the account information for you. Once you have entered the code, the company's information will appear on your banking site, and you can complete the payment. You will have a unique customer reference code so that they can cross-reference the payments. You will find the reference number next to the BPay code on your bill.

EFT

You will probably know that EFT stands for "Electronic Funds Transfer." You will be using your internet banking to make a once-off payment.

GOING TO THE DOCTOR

Doctors or General Practitioners (GPs)

This is a little different from how things work in other countries and will require one of those actions that you might think is complicated but really isn't.

You can walk into any medical centre, complete the new patient information paperwork and see a doctor or general practitioner (GP).

Walk-ins can wait for anything from ten minutes to an hour, and it is not considered impolite to ask the receptionist how long the wait will be. You will usually stick with this doctor if you are happy with him or her.

GPs in Australia perform many tasks that you would typically see a specialist for in your home country. They may perform minor surgeries in their rooms, and even gynaecological check-ups are performed by them.

You will require a referral note from a GP to see any specialist, for any tests, including blood tests and for X-rays.

The referral letter will include the contact details of the specialist. You will then need to phone the specialist's surgery to book your own appointment. Your GP is always your first port of call for anything.

Medicare
Medicare is Australia's "free" healthcare system. We say "free" because it is covered by the taxes we pay. Around 2% of tax is channelled towards the healthcare system.

Medicare is accessible to all Australian permanent residents, NZ residents and those who are from a country that has a reciprocal agreement with Australia. Unfortunately, not all countries have such an agreement. Unless you arrive as a permanent resident, you won't be able to access Medicare.

If you are eligible, you will need to go into a Medicare office and apply for the service. The application process will be discussed in more detail in Chapter 16.

You will often see this sign: "Bulk Billing". This means that the particular medical centre charges only the Medicare levy so you will not have any out of pocket expenses. Yes, when you have a Medicare card, you can visit a doctor or state hospital and not have to pay anything at the end of the consultation!

If you are entitled to Medicare and need to be referred to a specialist, then you can ask your doctor to refer you to a "Bulk Billing" specialist. It might mean you may have to wait a little longer for an appointment. Bulk billing can take a little longer than if you go to the private medical insurance route.

Many migrants have to take out private medical insurance upon arrival or for a visa anyway, so they tend to be in the habit of enjoying the speed of the private medical sector. You should reassess this a few years down the line, especially if you are perhaps being monitored for a particular condition. It could be worthwhile to go onto the public health system for the check-ups each year.

Your GP or specialist might be able to give you guidelines on the Medicare waiting times for the particular procedure you require.

It is worth mentioning that you should take out separate ambulance insurance. This is not necessarily a standard inclusion in your private medical insurance. Ambulance cover costs less than $100 per year for a family.

If you add ambulance cover to your standard insurance plan rather than taking out insurance directly with the ambulance service, there might be some exclusions – be sure to check the fine print.

For example, they might only cover you if your case is an "emergency" as declared by the paramedics. If you are only driven to hospital as a precaution, then your ambulance ride might not be covered.

Also, if you call an ambulance and the paramedics don't take you to hospital but treat you on the scene, you may not be covered. A ten-minute ride in an ambulance will set you back around $1 500. When treated on the scene, you can expect a bill of around $750.

For more information, visit the website:

www.servicesaustralia.gov.au/individuals/medicare

Chemist or pharmacy

In Australia, you are trusted to take your prescribed tablets up to the till to pay for them. They may sometimes be put into a container to make it easier to carry.

There are many pharmacies where you can set up automatic repeats to be dispensed as you need them, which is a very reliable service.

If the GP or specialist has given you a repeat prescription, you can hand it in at the pharmacy, with a few personal details like your telephone number, and the pharmacy will text you when the next script is due. You can also text back when you would like for it to be dispensed, and then just drop in to collect it.

Pharmaceutical Benefits Scheme

The Highly Specialised Drugs (HSD) program provides access to specialised Pharmaceutical Benefits Scheme (PBS) medicines for the treatment of chronic conditions.

These medicines, because of their clinical use and other special features, might have restrictions on where they may be prescribed and supplied.

To gain access to these drugs, a patient must:

- be an Australian resident and be eligible for a Medicare card,
- attend a participating hospital and be a day admitted patient, a non-admitted patient, or a patient on discharge, and
- be under appropriate specialist medical care and meet specific medical criteria.

For more information, visit the website:
www.servicesaustralia.gov.au/individuals/services/medicare/pharmaceutical-benefits-scheme

National Disability Insurance Scheme (NDIS)

From 1 July 2016, the **NDIS** is providing funding packages to more than 25 000 Australians under 65 who have a permanent impairment that substantially reduces their intellectual, cognitive, neurological, sensory, physical, psychological and social functioning. This also includes children with autism.

To be eligible for the NDIS you need to be:

- under 65 years when you apply,
- an Australian citizen or resident or permanent visa holder, and
- meet the disability or early intervention requirements.

For more information go to www.ndis.gov.au

SHOPPING

There are many ways to shop in Australia. Online shopping is the fastest growing industry here, and it is not unusual for some retailers to even offer same-day delivery. Most deliveries can be made within 48 hours. Australia's online shopping equates to around 60% of retail sales.

Strip/High street shops

If you are familiar with the United Kingdom's high street shopping, this is the same. It is a strip or row of shops central to the surrounding homes. These can vary in size from just a few essential services to a few kilometres of high street shopping brands.

Milk bar

The milk bar is a corner shop or local grocery shop where you can pick up a few supplies such as milk, bread, and sweets. Most milk bars these days supplement their income with a deep fryer, and you can buy take away meals, such as fish and chips, milkshakes, and coffee.

Regional shopping centre

The centre usually has one main anchor tenant, like a Coles or Woolworths, or a department store like Target or Kmart.

Outlet centres

These can be furniture and homeware centres or clothing centres, usually known as direct factory outlets (DFO). Some migrants may know these shops as "factory shops".

Opportunity shops

"Op shopping" is a big pastime in Australia. It is, in true Aussie-style, a shortened word for "opportunity shop", which is also known as a "thrift shop" or "charity shop".

People donate their unwanted or unused items to charity for resale. Op shopping is ideal for shopping for vintage clothing, or even high-end brand names that can be picked up for just a few dollars.

Op shops are treasure troves, and we can't recommend them highly enough for finding a few bargains. When you first arrive, you can buy toys, books, and DVD's aplenty!

Op shops are also great for buying kitchen items, such as crockery, cutlery, and small electrical items. You can also pick up linen, soft furnishings, lamps, and small furniture such as coffee tables, or even sofas and bed frames.

It really depends on what has been donated as to what you might find. Every town or village in Australia has at least one such shop. Look out for the following organisations' stores:

Shopping centres

The shopping malls (centres) in Australia are large, enclosed shopping areas from which traffic is excluded. In Australia, we mostly call them shopping centres, or by their local name, shortened of course. Chaddie (Chadstone) in Victoria is the biggest shopping centre in Australia.

There are big ones, small ones, modern ones, and older style ones, in fact, Australia is not far behind the USA and Canada when it comes to serving the most retail customers.

The biggest chain of shopping centres is called **Westfield**, which owns and manages around 40 centres across the country. Their website is www.westfield.com.au

Grocery shopping

You can take your shopping bags into a shop without a security guard waiting to check it or tape it closed. There are also very few stores who check your bag on departure.

The main grocery stores do not supply plastic bags; you need to buy "reusable bags" or bring your own bags.

Most grocery stores require either a $1 or $2 coin to unlock and access a trolley, which is refunded when you return the trolley into the trolley bay in the car park. If you don't have the correct coin, the information desk in the store will change money for you, or you can purchase a plastic token to use. Just keep the plastic token in your purse for easy access.

Vegetables and fruit are weighed at the checkout; you do not need to weigh them in the fresh produce area. Place your item in the small plastic bags provided, as you would normally do and when you unpack your trolley, the cashier will weigh them. In some stores there are scales to weigh items just for your information, so you can fine-tune your calculations if you like.

There is no "packer" waiting to pack your bags for you. The cashier will either pack your bags as the items are scanned, or they will be placed on the side for you to pack yourself.

There are self-service checkouts, and at most grocery stores you can withdraw money at the till or at the self-service checkout. Cashiers will ask if you want any "cash-out" before you make your final payment. The cash you want to withdraw is then added to your total shopping, and the cashier will give you the cash. Any amount from $10 to $200 is acceptable.

You might be asked for something like a "Flybuys" card several different shops because this card is linked to a variety of suppliers. You can earn Flybuys points at the grocery store, Coles, the department store, Kmart or any Shell service station (petrol station). You can also link it to your Virgin flight miles and even collect Flybuys from certain energy suppliers. They all offer Flybuy incentives.

More information on the **Coles Flybuys** and **Woolworths Rewards** incentive cards can be downloaded at the websites: www.flybuys.com.au and www.woolworthsrewards.com.au

When you are standing at the grocery cashier, there will be a little scanner nearby where you can scan your loyalty card while the cashier is busy with your groceries. You don't need to wait until everything has been scanned before producing your card.

The cashier may ask if you want your meat or cleaning products in a separate bag. Don't be irritated about this. Unlike in some countries, where your groceries are just randomly put into shopping bags, the Australians cashiers are considering your personal preferences.

We find that the cashiers in Australia are friendlier than most. You might be asked: "Having a good day?" and you can reply with a simple: "Yes, thank you." Some of them may be overly friendly and will even enquire if you "Got much on for the rest of the day?" A simple: "Ah, just back to work" or something similar is a sufficient reply. After your bags have been packed, they will be left on the side for you to load into your trolley. You do not tip the cashier for packing your bags.

It is local etiquette that you place the "produce divider" or "grocery separator" on the conveyer belt when loading your groceries. Don't expect the person behind you in the queue to have to reach over to retrieve it. When you have finished loading your groceries, place the divider for their convenience and as a statement that you have completed your load.

PUBLIC TRANSPORTATION

All cities have a reusable smart card that you will need to purchase for public transportation. They are usually around $6, and you can top it up at train/bus stations, some convenience stores and petrol stations.

There are a few reasons to use a smart card, namely:

1. **Online account management** – By downloading the app, you can manage your public transport card account online and see your current balance as well as view all journeys made and which method of transportation was used.

2. **More convenient** – When you use your public transport card, you simply 'tap on' and 'tap off' at the designated card readers at train stations, buses, light rail stops and ferry wharves. You don't have to try and find a ticket booth, and you don't have to waste time. If you're running late, you simply pull out your card and 'tap on'!

3. **Automatic top-up** – When your card balance goes lower than a specified amount (usually $5 for children or $10 for adults), the transit authority will automatically top it up via your debit card or credit card so that you can always use public transport. Of course, during the sign-up process, you need to provide permission for this function. You may also choose not to have automatic top-up and simply pay over the counter at various locations.

Most public transport runs from 4:30am to midnight, but this can vary. Major cities also have buses that run through the night, from a few key locations that are well lit and under CCTV surveillance. Here are the links for public transport and the capital cities which offer the reusable smart card system in each state:

1. **Australian Capital City:** In Canberra, they use **MyWay** on the buses, www.transport.act.gov.au

2. **New South Wales:** In Sydney they use the **Opal Card** system on trains, trams, buses and ferries - www.transportnsw.info

3. **Northern Territory:** Darwin uses the **Tap & Ride Card** on buses, www.nt.gov.au/driving/public-transport-cycling/public-buses/fares/tap-and-ride-card

4. **Queensland:** In Brisbane, the **Go Card** system works on trains, trams, buses, and ferries - www.translink.com.au

5. **South Australia:** Adelaide uses the **Metrocard** system on trains, trams, and buses - www.adelaidemetro.com.au

6. **Tasmania:** In Hobart, the **Greencard** is used on buses, www.metrotas.com.au

7. **Victoria:** Melbourne uses the **myki Card** system on trains, trams, and buses - www.ptv.vic.gov.au

8. **Western Australia:** Perth uses **SmartRider** on trains, buses, and ferries - www.transperth.wa.gov.au/SmartRider/Types-of-SmartRider

Safety and hygiene on public transportation

In general, Australia's public transportation systems are very well maintained and provide safe, clean services for customers. The systems are heavily regulated to ensure customers can rely on a high standard of facilities. It wouldn't be possible in Australia to see a train overloaded with passengers hanging out the windows or sitting on the roof, such as the case in other countries.

The trains, buses, trams, and ferries are modern and comfortable (mostly air-conditioned), and the stations and terminals looked after and monitored with 24-hour CCTV. Uniformed P.S.Os – Police Safety Officers and plain-clothed security guards patrol stations and terminals and at times, also ride on the vehicles to ensure the safety of all.

Public transportation in Australia is designed to be efficient, comfortable and safe. Be sure to purchase your smart card so that you can take advantage of every possible discount and special offer!

DRIVING IN AUSTRALIA

For some migrants arriving in Australia, driving is a real adjustment. In the ten years of relocating families, we've seen that it is an easy adjustment, but you just need to comply from day one – no negotiations! Slow down and be courteous, for your own safety and those of others.

In Australia, we have one of the lowest road death toll rates in the world – during 2017, there were only 1 224 deaths across the continent. That is not far off the same road death toll in England, of 1 710 – if you compare the land size and population, it provides reassurances that Australians are safe on the road, and the laws are respected and upheld.

The transport networks and rules and regulations vary

significantly from state to state. We encourage you to visit the website of both your state public transport service provider and the local road's website to check out the rules and regulations for your particular state/territory.

Generally, with some countries excluded, if you are arriving in Australia with a temporary work visa, you can drive with your current licence for the duration of your visa, provided that your current licence has not expired and that it is in English. If your licence is not in English, you will need to have this translated by a NAATI (www.naati.com.au) approved translation service. If you arrive as a permanent resident, then you have six months (varies in some states) to change your licence to comply with your local state. These rules do change frequently, so check regularly with your local state service provider. We have listed the licensing authorities below.

Most of the states have the learner driver's handbook available on their website. Download it and read it prior to your arrival. The book provides local legislation like rules for driving next to trams, alcohol and drug consumption laws and limits, and how the demerit points system works in your state or territory.

Here are the links for road and registrations in each state:

ACT	www.accesscanberra.act.gov.au
NSW	www.rms.nsw.gov.au
NT	www.mvr.nt.gov.au
QLD	www.qld.gov.au/transport/licensing
SA	www.sa.gov.au/topics/driving-and-transport
TAS	www.transport.tas.gov.au
VIC	www.vicroads.vic.gov.au
WA	www.transport.wa.gov.au

Below is an overview of the most important regulations. Remember that these rules and regulations vary between the states, so please check your local rules by following the links as listed above.

Blood Alcohol Concentration (BAC)

The blood alcohol concentration is a measurement of the amount of alcohol you have in your blood. It is measured by the grams of alcohol in 100 millilitres of blood. You should have a reading of less than 0.05 BAC, which is generally two standard glasses of wine.

Remember, you could still have alcohol in your blood the next morning after a party. Drivers admitted to hospital after any kind of road crash are required by law to allow blood samples to be taken.

If you are found to be over the limit, you will lose your licence for a minimum of six months for the first offence. For a reading higher than 0.10, a longer period will be imposed. Heavy penalty fines apply. Refusing a breath test is an offence. Your licence will be cancelled, and you will be disqualified from driving for at least two years.

Standard drinks guide

We've included this guide because a "standard drink" sometimes is not what you might be served in a restaurant or pub. Most often, the glasses are taller than a standard drink size – or the alcohol content is higher. Know your limits, and don't run the risk. In many drinking establishments, there is often a breathalyzer on a wall where you can test if you are still within the legal limits, but you should not be that close to the wire that you need to check this!

Number of standard drinks – beer	Number of standard drinks – wine
Full strength 4.8% alc. vol. 285 ml glass – 1.1 standard drinks 375 ml bottle or can – 1.4 standard drinks *Mid strength 3,5% alc. vol.* 285 ml glass – 0.8 standard drinks 375 ml bottle or can - 1 standard drink	*Red wine 13.5% alc. vol.* 100 ml standard serve - 1 standard drink 150 ml average restaurant serving – 1.6 standard drinks 750 ml bottle - 8 standard drinks

Number of standard drinks – beer	Number of standard drinks – wine
Low strength 2.7% alc. vol. 285 ml glass – 0.6 standard drinks 375 ml bottle or can – 0.8 standard drinks 425 ml glass – 0.9 standard drinks 24 x 375 ml case - 19 standard drinks	*White wine 11.5% alc. vol.* 100 ml standard serve - 1 standard drink 150 ml average restaurant serving – 1.4 standard drinks *Champagne 12.5% alc. vol.* 150 ml average restaurant serving – 1.5 standard drinks 750 ml bottle – 7.5 standard drinks *Port 17.5% alc. vol.* 60 ml standard serve – 0.8 standard drinks 2-litre cask - 28 standard drinks

Standard drinks guide

Seat belts

All passengers must wear a seat belt – including those in the back seat. Get your teenagers in the back seat used to this idea as soon as possible. We have seen many a stressed argument because backseat passengers won't put on their belts.

Babies under one year old are to be carried in an approved child restraint. Children up to 18 kilograms should be restrained in a suitable car seat. Booster seats are suitable for children between 14 kg and 26 kg. Please refer to Chapter 10 for more information.

Speed limits

Many migrants find driving here a little frustrating because it is so slow, but please stay well within the speed limits. The speed limit in built-up areas is 50 kilometres per hour (km/h) and is reduced to 40 km/h during peak school traffic times around schools and 60 km/h when the speed is usually 80 km/h or more.

Speed and red-light cameras are extremely common in

Australia. There are also speed cameras in unmarked cars parked on the side of the road. The speed limit on freeways and country roads is 100 km/h and 110 km/h on the Hume Freeway between Melbourne and Sydney.

Demerit points will be placed against your licence if you are caught speeding. This can range from one to six points, depending on the severity of the offence. For example, if you exceed the speed limit by more than 15 km/h but with less than 30 km/h, you will lose three demerit points.

If you get 12 demerit points within three years, your licence will be suspended. Depending on the circumstances, you will be set more stringent regulations before your licence is returned.

If you are caught more than 20 km over the speed limit, your car may be impounded for 30 days, and you will have to appear in court to determine your sentence and fine.

You should also know that in some states, on long weekends, there are double demit points for infringements.

If you are out on a country road, doing 80 km/h or 100 km/h and you enter a small town, you will need to brake and obey the 60 km/h limit. The car behind you will do the same. Trust us, some of the rural police officers are just waiting for you to keep going at 80 km/h through the town.

School zones

Migrant drivers are just about always caught off guard by the school speed zone restrictions. During school drop-off time (8am to 9:30am) and pick-up time (2:30pm and 4:00pm) the speed around school zones will be reduced by at least 20 km/h.

School zones are clearly indicated with signs, often accompanied by flashing lights, to remind motorists of this time of day.

If it is usually a 60 km zone, it will reduce to 40 km. You must have reduced speed by the time you reach the speed sign.

During this period, crossing supervisors, more commonly known as the "Lollypop man" or "Lollypop lady" can be seen in their fluorescent jackets, holding a crossing "STOP" sign.

Real-life story

I arrived in Australia from France and was used to driving on the right-hand side of the road, around the Arc d' Triomph – but not even that prepared me for the truck drivers in Australia! Trucks are allowed in the right-hand lane on the motorway, and they are not afraid to tailgate you with their double trailer semi rigs. I should point out that tailgating is an offence. These trucks can be quite daunting for any new arrival, but gratefully the road rules are being assessed, and there are trials underway to restrict trucks to the left-hand lanes.

Cities with trams

If you are going to be driving in a city with trams, it is strongly advised to familiarise yourself with the regulations regarding trams and rights of way in the city.

One of the most basic rules is that, if you are travelling alongside a tram and the tram stops, you must also stop. Trams travel in the right-hand lane of a dual road, so when they stop, you will be on their left. If you do not stop, you will knock over the pedestrians who need to cross your lane to reach the pavement. Cities with trams, such as Melbourne, will also have hook turns for those cars turning right to cross the tram line.

Hook turns

When driving in the city of Melbourne, it is critical to know how to do a hook turn. Visit the RACV website to watch a short video to explain the hook turn:
www.racv.com.au/on-the-road/driving-maintenance/road-safety/road-rules/making-turns.html

Parking

Remember to park your car facing the direction in which you are travelling!

Jaywalking

With caution, you can cross the road at a pedestrian crossing and the cars will stop, you have the right of way. If you choose to cross the road anywhere else, and you are jaywalking, you could receive an "on the spot" fine, especially during peak traffic times, for not obeying the rules.

Cycling

There are dedicated cycle lanes in the cities and suburbs. In Sydney, failure to wear a helmet will result in a fine of anything between $50 for children to $300 for adults in Sydney. Remember, each state differs. There are also fines for cyclists who run red lights or do not stop for pedestrians at a pedestrian crossing.

Taxis

There are several taxi companies you can call or hail from the roadside. Prices may vary, but usually, they are:
1. $3,20 starting meter when hailed,
2. $1,62 per kilometre, and
3. $2 booking charge.

Additional charges apply for toll routes, airport transfers, and when travelling on toll roads.

Taxi fare calculator:
Use this link to **calculate** a taxi fare: www.taxifare.com.au
1. Download the mobile phone app for 13cabs' on www.13cabs.com.au
2. Download the mobile phone app for Silvertop Taxi's on www.silvertop.com.au/app/

Safe city taxi ranks:
Most cities have safe city taxi ranks in the CBD to give patrons, and taxi drivers access to safe transport late at night. Uniformed security officers are present at each taxi rank. Safe city cameras monitor the ranks during their hours of operation:

1. From midnight on Fridays to 6am on Saturdays, and
2. From midnight on Saturdays to 6am on Sundays, each weekend of the year and during special events such as the Melbourne Grand Prix weekend and New Year's Eve.

Toll roads

Toll roads in Australia work well and are efficient. You will be invoiced if you have not set up an account. If you do not pay your invoice, you will receive a fine for each day travelled without making a payment. This could end up being around $114 per day.

When you apply for your toll account, you will have an eTag posted to you. This is fixed to your car's windscreen, and each time you pass under the motorway gantry, the eTag will beep. If it beeps more than once, then your account needs credit added or there is a problem with the eTag.

Set up your account online, receive your eTag and set up an automatic top-up of your account (you can set this amount). Once your credit falls below the set amount, it will automatically deduct the same amount from your bank account.

Check your local city information to find out about tolls in your area. If you have travelled on a toll road, you will have three days to go online and make a payment before an invoice is issued.

SMOKING

You will find that smoking in Australia is very expensive, so if you ever needed a reason to quit, now is the time! At the time of writing this book, a basic packet of 25 cigarettes cost around $36. Premium brands cost around $55.

Besides the price, there are strict laws in place about smoking. Maybe that is why there is a very steady decline in smokers in Australia.

Also refer to Chapter 10 for more information on smoking regulations.

LOCAL LIFE AND CULTURE

When we compare all the countries we have lived in, Australia is still the best. You can pursue just about any dream, any sport, and any hobby. There is always an event going on, a farmers' or craft market, a music festival, picnic in the botanical gardens, a beachfront funfair, a cycle race, or marathon around the city. Embrace it all; you will love it!

Barbecues

"Barbies", as they are best known in Australia, are always a popular form of outdoor dining and socialising. It is centralised around cooking meat on an open fire or gas fire. They are informal, often spontaneous, and enjoyable. It is not unusual to be told to "bring a plate", this means you should bring a plate of finger food to be eaten while the meat is on the "barbie". Most often, you will bring your own meat and drinks, and the host will provide salads and snacks. You should always ask the host what to bring, just to clarify.

Religion

The 2016 National census revealed that around 61% of the Australian population is affiliated with a religion or spiritual belief. Christianity is the dominant religion, with support of around 12 million people.

According to the census, the next group is those who indicated "No religion", followed by Islam and then Buddhism. Around 30% of Australians indicated "No religion" on their census; this was an increase of almost 50% from the 2011 census. Here are some websites to consider in your search:

Christian affiliations:
- Reformed Churches (www.crca.org.au)
- Presbyterian Churches (www.presbyterian.org.au)
- Uniting Churches (www.assembly.uca.org.au)
- Lutheran Churches (www.lca.org.au)

- Baptist Churches (www.baptist.org.au)
- Pentecostal Churches (www.acc.org.au)
- Churches of Christ (www.cofcaustralia.org)
- Anglican Churches (www.anglican.org.au)
- Catholic Churches (www.catholic.org.au)
- Jehovah Witnesses (www.jw.org/en/)
- 7Th Day Adventists (www.adventist.org.au)

Other religious affiliations:
- Jewish synagogues (www.jewishaustralia.com)
- Buddhist temples (www.buddhistcouncil.org.au)
- Hindu temples (www.hinducouncil.com.au)
- Sikh gurdwaras (www.sikhhelpline.com.au)
- Islamic mosques or centres (www.afic.com.au)

Sea, sun and surf

The surf around Australia can be just as dangerous as in other parts of the world, so the same rules apply. Always swim between the red and yellow flags!

When it comes to protecting yourself from the Aussie sun, our mascot, Sid the seagull, says:

"Slip, Slop, Slap, Seek & Slide"

1. Slip on sun-protective clothing that covers as much of your body as possible.

2. Slop on SPF 30 or a higher, broad-spectrum, water-resistant sunscreen, at least 20 minutes before sun exposure. Reapply every two hours when outdoors or more often if perspiring or swimming.

3. Slap on a broad-brimmed hat that shades your face, neck and ears.

4. Seek shade.

5. Slide on sunglasses.

Children, especially those in primary school, will have to wear compulsory sun hats, will have to carry sunscreen and sports will be cancelled under the extreme weather policy.

The anti-cancer council recommends that everybody uses a sunscreen with SPF 50+ during summer. Try to stay in the shade between 11am and 3pm, as this is when the sun is at its strongest. More information regarding being "sun smart" visit: www.cancer.org.au

Sports

Given the rich history of the first migrants to set foot on Australian soil, there is an abundance of sports and recreational activities in Australia.

Depending on which state or territory you live in, you will be exposed to different levels of popularity.

In NSW, for example, you'll find the Rugby Union (Springboks and Wallabies), Queenslanders love their Rugby League, and everybody loves the Australian Football League (AFL), especially Victorians, as Victoria is the birthplace of footy (AFL).

In Australia, the number for an average weekly support crowd for a game of Rugby Union or AFL (footy) is supported by well over 40 000 people every week! The 2017 AFL final attracted 100 021 spectators.

Sports in Australia is well-supported. In Victoria, there even is a public holiday on the Friday prior to the Footy Grand Finals, so there can be a footy parade through the city. Victoria also shuts down for a public holiday for the Melbourne Cup Horserace.

Cricket is one of the longest-standing sports in Australia. The first cricket club was founded in Melbourne in the early

1800s, along with horseracing, soccer, and golf. Soccer is the fastest growing sport now in Australia. The early roots of AFL commenced around 1859.

These are just the main branches of sport. There is a great focus now on women's sports, with new clubs for women's AFL, cricket, and rugby. That's not to say that men's netball is not a growing sport either.

As already mentioned, the early settlers to Australia embedded a gambling trait that is a thriving industry in sports today. In fact, the first betting can be found in the history books as early as 1840. Even though gambling was illegal until 1980, around 80% of Australians still engage in betting. It is a national pastime. Don't be surprised if there is some sort of social betting even taking place around your offices, too.

You will find some great interactive sports museums, especially in Canberra and Melbourne. If you do find yourself in either city, a tour is a must. Take the kids, it is fully interactive, and you will have a great day out www.australiansportsmuseum.org.au

Australian Football League (AFL)

As this sport is such an institution in Australian life, you should familiarize yourself with it. You may be not familiar with AFL. We do encourage you to go to a game and experience the passion. You will also see much more of the ball action than on TV.

Remember around 40 000 people will attend a footy match! In Melbourne, most supporters will even meet at Federation Square and walk to the stadium in their thousands, often chanting their team song!

Melbourne is home to AFL, which was born in Victoria and is often referred to as VFL (Victorian Football League). If you want to take part in conversations at work, you will need to learn the game, choose a team, and have fun!

The Australian Football League (AFL) is the premier sports competition in Australia, commanding high levels of corporate sponsorship, massive media coverage for twelve months of the year with huge game attendance. AFL Football is one of the largest sectors in Australia's sport and recreational industry. Defined as an industry, the game employs about 5 000 people.

Real-life story
At my first job in Australia, I was introduced to all my new colleagues in the office. Their second question after the introduction was: "Who do you barrack for?" meaning "Who do you support?"

Most migrants' default reply usually is:
> *"I don't like sport", or*
> *"I watch soccer or cricket", or*
> *"I don't like Footy. I am a rugby supporter."*

Don't be surprised to get a cold shoulder or indifference from your new colleagues. Just pick an AFL team and hop onto the footy bus. I chose the Geelong Cats because I like cats. Don't overthink it, just pick a random AFL team and start your first Australian working day on the right foot.

Here is a brief overview of the game:

Team players
Eighteen players on the ground and four on the interchange bench.

The rules
The basic skills are kicking, marking, and handballing and umpires ensure that the transfer of the ball occurs fairly. Teams attempt to gain maximum points during the game.

The AFL laws
A player with the ball may be tackled above the knees and below the neck only.

A player may be bumped or shepherded only if the ball is within five meters.

A mark may be paid only when the football travels at least

10 meters, untouched, and is controlled by the recipient without touching the ground.

A goal is scored only if the ball is kicked, untouched, through the two tall posts at either end of the ground.

A handball is legal only if the ball is held in one hand and hit by the other with a clenched fist.

Scoring:
A goal shall register six points and a behind one point.

Mark:
A mark is awarded for catching the ball directly from the kick of another player, not less than ten meters distant, the ball being held for a reasonable time and not having been touched in transit from kick to catch.

Handball:
A player must hold the ball in one hand and hit it with the clenched fist of the other hand. If the ball is not handballed correctly, a free kick will be given to the nearest opponent.

Kick:
Contact must be below the knee.

Ball possession:
A player may hold the ball for any length of time, provided he is not held by an opponent. If he runs with the ball, he must bounce it or touch it on the ground at least once within every 15 meters from the start of his run, whether running in a straight line or turning and dodging.

Free kicks:
The player who makes the ball his sole objective will be given every opportunity to gain possession of the ball. The player who has possession of the ball and is held by an opponent will be given a reasonable time to kick or handball the ball. The ball will be kept in motion.

Current AFL clubs

Club	Nickname	State	Stadium
Adelaide	Crows	SA	Adelaide Oval
Brisbane	Lions	QLD	The Gabba
Carlton	Blues	VIC	Docklands Stadium
Collingwood	Magpies	VIC	MCG
Essendon	Bombers	VIC	Docklands Stadium
Fremantle	Dockers	WA	Perth Stadium
Geelong	Cats	VIC	Kardinia Park
Gold Coast	Suns	QLD	Carrara Stadium
Greater Western Sydney	Giants	NSW	Sydney Showground
Hawthorn	Hawks	VIC	MCG
Melbourne	Demons	VIC	MCG
North Melbourne	Kangaroos	VIC	Docklands Stadium
Port Adelaide	Power	SA	Adelaide Oval
Richmond	Tigers	VIC	MCG
St Kilda	Saints	VIC	Docklands Stadium
Sydney	Swans	NSW	SCG
West Coast	Eagles	WA	Perth Stadium
Western Bulldogs	Bulldogs	VIC	Docklands Stadium

SUMMARY OF RECOMMENDATIONS

1. Familiarise yourself with the state laws specific to the state where are you settling.

2. Get ambulance cover.

3. Download the learner driver's handbook for each state.

4. Familiarise yourself with public transport options in your city.

5. Choose a footy team – especially if you live and work in Melbourne.

7

AUSTRALIAN ETIQUETTE

"Manners are a sensitive awareness of the feelings of others.
If you have that awareness, you have good manners, no matter what
fork you use."

~ *Emily Post*
(Etiquette and manners expert)

Ever wondered what is and isn't good etiquette in Australia? Well, fear not, you have a little leeway because Australians don't have too many rigid and unbreakable rules.

However, there is always a code of conduct, an unwritten rule of what makes people feel comfortable. In this chapter, we are only listing a few, but this is definitely not the ultimate list.

PERSONAL SPACE

Australia is the ninth least densely populated country in the world. People, therefore, have a fairly large personal space. It is considered rude to brush up against someone unless it's absolutely necessary (like on a crowded bus or train).

When there is enough space available, try to stay at an arm's length from people. If you have to invade that space for some reason, an "excuse me" or "sorry" is appropriate. Unless there's assigned seating, or a theatre is completely full, leave a couple of chairs open between you and a stranger.

GREETING AND SAYING HELLO

Just saying "Hello!" and making eye contact is fine. A handshake may be appropriate if you're meeting someone with whom you expect to have an ongoing relationship, such as a new work colleague. Even in formal situations, Australians tend to prefer first names. Addressing someone (even your boss) as "Mister" or "Miss", "Sir" or "Ma'am" can sound a bit stiff.

If an Australian decides to hug or kiss you, let them take the initiative. Women will greet other women with a kiss and a hug, and shoulder hug their male friends. Men don't tend to be physically demonstrative with other men unless they are very firm friends or family members. A handshake is fine. Maintain good eye contact, but without staring.

Receiving a compliment should be acknowledged with a "thank you". This is something migrants often struggle with, and upon receipt of a compliment might reply: "Oh, this old thing, I got it..." Not accepting a compliment may be perceived as rejection, and you may never get another compliment from that person.

It goes without saying that speaking a language other than English in the company of Australians is deemed rude. They won't understand what you are saying and might think that you are mocking them or gossiping. The same goes for whispering in public – it is not good manners.

THE LEFT, TO THE LEFT...

Australians drive on the left-hand side of the road, and this convention was also adopted in other areas of Australian life.

When you are stopping on an escalator or walking upstairs, always stick to the left and don't block other people from passing you by resting your hand on the right-side railing. This rule also applies to escalators in supermarkets or shopping centres. Make sure that you and your shopping trolley are stationed to the left of the escalators.

Equally, when walking on the sidewalk, try to keep left where possible. Pay special attention when walking on special bike roads, where it's not just a matter of politeness, but also a matter of safety to keep left.

ELEVATORS

Australians call them both "elevators" and "lifts" but the rules are simple. It's polite to hold the doors for people who are approaching the elevator. It's also polite to ask which floor the person would like to go to if you are standing closest to the buttons, especially if it's crowded and they may find it hard to reach over.

DOORS

If someone is within five steps of a door when you're walking through it, hold it open for the person. There are no special rules for males or females, simply hold doors for people who are near and maybe make an extra allowance for someone carrying something. And remember, a "thank you" for their consideration goes a long way.

QUEUES

In some cultures, queuing is optional. In Australia, the queue is sacred. Jumping the queue in any situation – at a bar, a service desk or C, it is considered the utmost rudeness.

Most of the time, it's pretty obvious where a queue begins and ends, but if you're in any doubt, simply ask: "Excuse me, is this the end of the line?"

It is not unusual if the person behind you at the grocery store only has a few items to let that person go ahead of you. The same applies to an elderly person, pregnant women, or somebody with small children.

If you're in a crowded place, like a nightclub or the deli-queue at the supermarket, pay special attention to who was waiting at the bar to be served before you. If an attendant approaches you instead of someone who was there before you, it's polite to signal that the other person was there first. At some counters, there is a little machine where you take a number and wait until your number is called out.

RESPIRATORY HYGIENE AND GROOMING

In Australia, it is common practice to be more conscious of proper respiratory hygiene.

If you're coughing or sneezing, use a disposable tissue and if there's none available, cough or sneeze into the inner elbow rather than into your hand.

Spitting in public places is a big no-no, and public urination is considered an offence in Australia.

It is also not acceptable to perform any grooming in public – picking teeth, cleaning nails, squeezing spots.

PUBLIC TRANSPORTATION

If you're waiting to board public transport, be sure to wait for everyone to exit before you try to get on. Not waiting for people to exit first is something that will definitely irritate other travellers, especially early on a Monday morning.

Top tip: *If the train or bus is full during the morning peak hour, move to the centre of the carriage or bus and stand next to school children who are seated. One would hope that they will give up their seat for you, but in any event, they will get off at one point, and you could slide into a seat.*

Talking on a cell phone (known as a mobile in Australia) on public transport is tolerated but try to keep your voice down. If you are only taking a short journey, rather call the person back.

In Sydney, Brisbane, Melbourne and a few other capital cities, peak hour traffic on public transport is under strain, and it's easy to get on other people's nerves.

Check out the insider guides.com website for more public transport etiquette.

USING A TAXI

When you are travelling alone, and you are using a taxi, you are supposed to sit in the front seat. The back seat feels too much like one is being chauffeured, and it is difficult to have a conversation with the driver. Taxi drivers around the world identify Aussies by this trait!

LITTERING

In 1979, when NASA's Skylab space station came crashing down in Western Australia, the sleepy town of Esperance issued NASA a $400 fine for littering. Australians take a lot of pride in the state of their environment, and while it is not as clean as in Singapore, littering is not just an affront, but it is also illegal.

Since the late 1960s, most Australians have grown up with the slogan: "Do the right thing – put it in the bin." This extends to indoors as well as outdoors. When eating in a food hall, or anywhere where tables and chairs are shared, take your rubbish to the bin when you are finished. In fact, if you can see any bins, it's a sign that you're expected to use them. Clean up after yourself! Even in places like cinemas, where people are paid to clean up after you, it's polite to drop your empty popcorn boxes in the bin on the way out. Never, ever, drop litter or cigarette butts outside!

INTERACTING WITH SERVICE STAFF

Australians have a strong culture of egalitarianism that they don't like to see violated. No matter what a person's job is, treat people with equal respect and use "please", "thank you" and "excuse me". Never snap your fingers, whistle, or yell at service staff to get their attention. As well as being considered rude, the standard of service you will receive may drop as a result.

DINING OUT OR DINNER PARTIES

If a group of friends or colleagues go to a restaurant, the bill will automatically be split amongst all the diners. It is unlikely that one individual will feel an obligation to pay for the others, nor do any of the other members of the dining party expect or want to be paid you to pay for by someone else.

To accept this generosity may evoke feelings of shame that one is a "bludger" (a person who avoids working, a loafer, a hanger-on, one who does not pull his weight). However, if it is a business dinner, one person may pay to foster goodwill among the rest.

At a dinner party, wine is the appropriate alcoholic contribution made by guests. At the end of the party, it is etiquette to leave any leftover wine as a gift for the host/s.

There is an Australian saying that when hosting a barbecue, a knock on the door should never be answered, as it means the guest isn't carrying the required case of beer. (One should only answer a kick on the door!)

If invited to someone's home for a barbecue, etiquette stipulates that you make a contribution to the alcohol that will be drunk. If bringing beer, a six-pack is okay, but a case of beer is more appropriate.

Depending on the nature of the barbecue, sometimes etiquette allows for leftover unopened beers to be taken home. But if the host has provided a large banquet, it is good manners to leave beers for the host as a gesture of thanks.

If a BBQ is extremely informal, the guests may also be asked to bring their own meat. Sometimes people get away with just bringing a potato salad or pavlova. Always be courteous enough to check with the host or hostess if they would like you to bring something before you arrive at the party. It is always kind to offer help to the host/hostess with preparing a meal or cleaning up after the party.

TIPPING

Tipping is optional in Australia. In restaurants, a tip is only left if above-average service has been delivered. Service staff get good salaries, so they don't rely on tips to survive. Some migrants are used to tip as a means to provide feedback on the level of service received. This is not common in Australia.

Taxi drivers are usually only tipped if they initiate a good conversation and don't rip off their customers. Bar staff members are usually not tipped, and they will continue to serve you on your subsequent visits without holding a grudge.

MAKING CONVERSATION

There aren't many taboo topics in Australia, although if you've just met someone, you might want to avoid topics of race, religion, politics and sex until you know them better. If you're looking for sure and safe conversation starters, try the weather or sports (especially football).

MOBILE PHONES

To be without your mobile phone these days can feel like you have lost a limb! There is a time and place for phones, though. You should not use your phone in the restroom, on public transport or any other place where you are confined to a small space, and people have no option but to listen to your conversation.

Please don't talk on the phone while checking out at a hotel or paying for groceries. Swearing is never polite in public, so watch your language while you're on the phone. Never choose your phone over someone you are already talking to in the room.

JOKES AND HUMOUR

Around the world, most jokes are based on some or other derogatory theme. To avoid offending the victim's feelings, most nationalities usually only tell the joke when its victim is not present. In Australia, this can be a risky thing to do. Some Australians don't like people joking about groups, if you are not part of that group. Instead of laughing, they might get angry and call the joke teller a "bigot".

Australians prefer to tell a derogatory joke when the victim of the joke is present. For example, when an Australian meets a New Zealander on holiday, they may ask if the person brought Velcro gloves to get a better grip on those Australian sheep.

"Taking the piss" is the term used for making a joke about someone or an ethnic group when that person or ethnic group is present.

If you are offended by Australians making jokes about someone or your ethnic group, it is best to smile and change the topic. Showing that your feelings got hurt, may simply motivate the Australian to tell another similar joke. Getting angry and threatening the person may result in the Australian taking you up on your offer!

If you are teased, you are expected to reply in kind and with good humour. Such self-confidence will increase an Australian's respect for you. They do not admire a subservient attitude.

Australians generally have a misplaced sense of humour. While telling a joke or labelling somebody, they might say something and mean quite the opposite.

They will take delight in dubbing a tall man "Shorty", a silent one "Rowdy", a bald man "Curly" and a redhead "Blue". A "bastard" may mean a good bloke. Likewise, "larrikin", "wog", and "mongrel" may all be used as terms of endearment.

TIME

Different cultures have different relationships with time. Like many Anglo-Saxon cultures, Australians have a linear relationship with time. That simply means that time is measured by the clock.

It is important to arrive on time for an appointment and even be a few minutes early, especially in business situations.

Make sure to respect business hours (9am-5pm). This includes emails and messages unless it's a matter of urgency. However, when invited to someone's home for a social event, it's best not to arrive exactly on time, but a little later (no more than 15 minutes).

HONESTY

It may seem strange for a society that stems from a group of convicts, but Australians really value honesty. It is acceptable to pull someone's leg or play a joke, but on serious issues, honesty is the best policy.

This is reflected in sayings such as: "poor but honest", "fair dinkum", "honest toiler", "honesty of substance" and "having an honest crack".

Many Australians are quite cynical and almost seem to view strangers as "guilty" until they prove themselves otherwise. Perhaps this is why buying your round at the pub is such an important thing to do. It shows that you are not out for all you can get.

Australians are difficult to impress. Even if you do manage to impress them, they may not openly admit it.

MATESHIP

There are several explanations for and interpretations of the Australian "mateship" concept.

"Mate" is a gender-neutral term, more commonly used by men than by women. It carries with it a sense of obligation to do the right thing as seen by one's close friends.

Mates in Australia serve the role that family members serve in other countries. Mates can be relied upon in times of need and will stand by you through the good times and the bad. This can be attributed to Australia's history as a migrant nation. Convicts, orphans, prostitutes, and lone individuals came to Australia without families. Consequently, their friends substituted their family network.

Another explanation is that it came from the hardships of the first century. It has long been known in psychological circles that social bonding coincides with extreme difficulty. (For this reason, defence force training inflicts hardship upon new recruits to foster such bonding.) The hardships endured by convicts and farmers caused them to feel a great sense of reliance upon each other.

A final explanation is that it stems from Australia's wars being fought on foreign territory. When a digger was dying, a mate was brought to stand next to him so he wouldn't die alone. Australia has never engaged in a war on home territory.

When men died, they often died with their families. When men survived, they often saw their wives, children and grandparents raped and killed. Accordingly, Australians' scars of war were of a different nature than that of other nations.

CHILDREN AND TEENS

We are not going to remind you that "Please" and "Thank you" are expected or that you should eat with your mouth closed. Here are some Australian expectations, so that you know. If you have visitors, the children are expected to come and greet the guests, not necessarily immediately, but in good time. They should also come to the door to say goodbye.

When children are visiting others, they should always take their plate to the kitchen and thank the host. If you are eating out, most children above the age of five years are expected to order their own food. Yes, mommies, don't try to organise them and order on their behalf!

BUSINESS ETIQUETTE AND CUSTOMS

Relationships and communication

1. Australians are very matter of fact when it comes to business, so they do not need long-standing personal relationships before they do business with people.
2. Australians are very direct in the way they communicate. There is often an element of humour, often self-deprecating, in their speech. Aussies often use colourful language that would be unthinkable in other countries.

Business meeting etiquette

1. Appointments are necessary and relatively easy to schedule. They should be made with as much lead time as possible.
2. Punctuality is important in business situations. It is better to arrive early than to keep someone waiting.
3. Meetings are generally relaxed; however, they are serious events.

4. If an Australian takes exception to something that you say, they will tell you so.
5. If you make a presentation, avoid hype, making exaggerated claims, or bells and whistles. Present your business case with facts and figures. Emotions and feelings are not important in the Australian business climate.

Negotiating and decision making

1. Australians get down to business quickly with a minimum amount of small talk.
2. They are quite direct and expect the same in return. They appreciate brevity and are not impressed by too much detail.
3. Negotiations proceed quickly. Bargaining is not customary. They will expect your initial proposal to have only a small margin for negotiation.
4. They do not like high-pressure techniques.
5. Decision making is concentrated at the top of the company, although decisions are made after consultation with subordinates, which can make decision-making slow.

Business attire

1. In Melbourne and Sydney, business attire is conservative. Men wear a dark, traditional business suit, especially for an interview or first meeting.
2. Women wear a smart dress or a business suit (usually black with a white blouse).
3. In Brisbane or other tropical areas, depending on the job and company culture, men may wear shirts and Bermuda shorts.

Business cards

Business cards are exchanged at the initial introduction without formal ritual. If you are not given a business card, it is not an insult; the person simply may not have one.

Stage three of culture shock is the Adjustment Stage.

8

CULTURE SHOCK

"Every country is like a particular type of person. America is like a belligerent, adolescent boy; Canada is like an intelligent, 35-year-old woman. Australia is like Jack Nicholson. It comes right up to you and laughs very hard in your face in a highly threatening and engaging manner."

~ Douglas Adams
(Author of The Hitchhiker's Guide to the Galaxy)

We briefly mentioned this phenomenon in the first chapter. Culture shock is the experience people have when they move from their own, familiar cultural environment to another culture which is different and unfamiliar.

It also refers to the personal disorientation a person feels when experiencing an unfamiliar way of life due to immigration, a visit to a new country, a move between social environments, or simply a transition to another type of life.

WHAT IS CULTURE SHOCK?

Until 1960, culture shock was assumed to be a consistently negative experience, much like an illness or disease. The Canadian anthropologist, Kalervo Oberg, who popularised the term, described it in simple terms as the "anxiety that results from losing all of your familiar signs and symbols of social intercourse".

What are your familiar signs or cues? It includes a thousand and one different ways in which we orientate ourselves to the situations of daily life, without thinking about it:

Familiar places

You know street names, friends' addresses, the school drive, where your bank is, where you get the freshest vegetables and the best bread in town. You know your pharmacist by name, or your GP has known you since you were born.

Familiar cues

You know how and when to shake hands, how to accept or refuse invitations or when to take a statement seriously or not. It also includes cues concerning customs and norms, for example introducing your life partner as your husband. You know how to interpret hand gestures and body language, and you know who to avoid, like the town gossips or toxic people.

Personal values

Values that you have considered to be good, desirable, beautiful, and valuable are no longer respected by the hosts in the new country. Or what you believed to be your strong personality traits might suddenly be your weakest traits.

The above-mentioned familiar cues and values are part of our daily unconscious awareness, our comfort zone. You don't think about these things; they just happen automatically.

In psychology, the four stages of competence, or the "conscious competence" learning model, relate to the psychological states involved in the process of progressing from incompetence to competence in a skill.

When you enter a strange or new culture, all your unconscious or familiar cues are removed. You are like a fish out of water. No matter how open-minded and prepared you are, you will have feelings of frustration and anxiety.

Culture shock is a very individual process and is dependent on intrapersonal factors such as age, previous travel experiences, language skills, resourcefulness, independence, resilience, health, and a support network.

THE STAGES OF CULTURE SHOCK

Oberg further identified culture shock consisting of at least one of four distinct stages:

- honeymoon,
- negotiation,
- adjustment, and
- adaptation.

Emotions that go up and down during these stages are commonly referred to as the "W-curve" or "Rollercoaster ride" of culture shock.

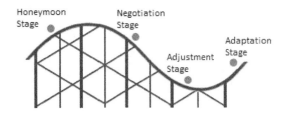

The honeymoon stage

During the honeymoon stage, the differences between the old and the new culture are seen in a romantic light. This stage may last from a few days or weeks to several months.

Most newly arrived migrants are in awe of the new freedom they have, how easy it is to connect utilities, the phenomenon of safe public transport, the cleanliness of the suburbs and how polite motorists are.

You may feel euphoric and be pleased with all the new things you encounter. This stage is also called "blissful ignorance". At this stage, you are unaware of cultural differences. It does not occur to you that you may be making cultural mistakes or that you may be misinterpreting much of the behaviour going on around you.

Your fascination with the new culture will make you more open to engaging with other migrants and friendly Australians. However, like any honeymoon, this stage eventually ends.

The negotiation (or anxiety) stage

After about three to six months, depending on the individual, differences between the old and new culture become apparent and may create anxiety, confusion, and irritation.

The excitement eventually gives way to frustration and anger as you continue to experience unfavourable events that may be perceived as strange and offensive to your cultural attitude.

According to Oberg, a sure sign of culture shock is when foreigners in another country get together to grumble and groan about their new country and its people.

You now realize that differences do exist between the way you and the local people behave, though you understand very little about what these differences are, how numerous they might be, or how deep they might go. You know there is a problem here, but you're not sure about the size of it. You're not so sure of your instincts anymore, and you realize that there are some things you don't understand.

You may start to worry about how hard it's going to be to figure these people out.

Many migrants have issues with language barriers (if non-English speaking), stark differences in moral values (swearing, blasphemy, gambling, religion, body piercing and tattoos), the quality and availability of home-country specific food. These issues and the constant confrontation of your moral values may heighten your sense of disconnection from your new surroundings.

Being transferred to a different environment also puts special pressure on your body. You will experience the 24-hour body rhythm disruption that often leads to insomnia and daylight drowsiness, the adaptation of gut flora to different bacteria levels and concentrations in food and water, and the adjustment to country-specific pollen (wattle trees).

You will have difficulties in seeking treatment for illnesses (as medicines have different names in Australia) and you will find that some active ingredients, like codeine phosphate, found in an opioid analgesic or painkiller, may be illegal in Australia.

Still, the most important change in this stage is communication. People adjusting to a new culture often feel lonely and homesick because they are not yet used to the new environment and meet new people every day.

The language barrier may be a major obstacle in creating new relationships. Special attention must be paid to your own and others' culture-specific body language signs, linguistic faux pas (embarrassing moments), conversational tone, linguistic nuances and customs, and "false friends" (words in two languages that look or sound familiar, but differ significantly in meaning, for example, "breed" – see Chapter 11).

The biggest source of irritation can stem from Australians and more settled migrants who seem mostly disinterested in your struggles. They will try to help, but they are just not getting it. It feels like they are unsympathetic, unaware, and uninformed about migration issues. A big obstacle could be to connect with your fellow countrymen who are already settled in Australia. You may perceive them as indifferent or feel that they don't want to deal with the "newbies'" issues because you are still too "fresh off the boat" (FOB) for their company.

Most migrants, however, are doing their best, and some just don't have the emotional aptitude or headspace to assist new migrants.

This part of the negotiation stage is particularly important and potentially disastrous. Everything that is from your country of origin may be irrationally glorified, and only the good things are remembered, like the great housekeeper, or how good the local bakery was who served the best vanilla slices.

Other than glorifying the good things, Oberg warns that this part can become disastrous if you "take refuge in the migrant colony of your countrymen and its cocktail circuit (party or social circuit) which often becomes the fountain-head ("breeding place") of emotionally charged labels known as stereotypes" such as "these bloody Aussies are such and so".

The use of stereotypes might soften your bruised ego, but it is just another sign of someone with a severe case of culture shock. If you overcome it, you stay in Australia; if not, you leave, or you could have major mental health issues later on.

You may think that it is better to avoid your fellow countrymen completely. Maybe you are tired of negative countrymen who always find problems instead of providing solutions.

However, migrants who avoid contact with their own countrymen, who are already settled Australians, develop additional symptoms of loneliness that ultimately could affect their lifestyles as a whole. Living in a new country without any social support will leave you more anxious than those who initially connect with other migrants.

You will experience a feeling of inner peace, a place of tranquillity where you can relax and enjoy the company of your fellow countrymen. They are more "like-minded" and understand your sense of humour. While you may have many Australian friends, it is just different in a good way when you are with other migrants of your own kind.

The adjustment (or recovery) stage

During this stage, usually between six to twelve months, individuals accept an objective view of their experience. They choose to become "explorers" of the new culture and attractions in the new country. They have an increased ability and a balanced perspective to see the bad and good elements in both the previous home and the new host culture.

You finally reach the stage where you realise that you need to re-evaluate your high expectations and that it is going to take more time than you anticipated.

You realize cultural differences exist, you know what some of these differences are, and you try to adjust your own behaviour accordingly. It doesn't come naturally yet — you have to make a conscious effort to behave in culturally appropriate ways — but you are much more aware of how your behaviour is coming across to the local people. You are in the process of replacing old instincts with new ones. You know now that you will be able to figure these people out if you can remain objective.

Migrants will find that they feel more relaxed and the unnatural fight or flight mode that was subconsciously part of their everyday life is slowly but surely starting to fade – like a weight being lifted off their shoulders.

Oberg states that during this stage, your sense of humour will return, and you will start cracking jokes about your situation. You will realise there is always another person who is worse off than yourself.

You start to appreciate your newly gained freedom, realizing what it should be like in a normal society. Even very sceptical migrants become more positive and hopeful about the future. Teenagers who didn't want to migrate, all of a sudden become more optimistic, not feeling that urgent need to return to their home country anymore.

There are three basic outcomes of this phase:

1.   Some migrants find it **impossible to accept** the foreign culture and to integrate. They isolate themselves from the host country's environment, which they come to perceive as hostile, withdraw into an (often mental) "ghetto" and view returning to their own culture as the only way out.

2.   Some migrants **integrate fully** and take on all parts of the host culture while losing their original identity. This is called cultural assimilation. They usually remain in the host country forever.

3. Some migrants **manage to adapt** to the aspects of the host culture they see as positive while keeping some of their own and creating their own unique cultural blend.

They have no significant problems returning home or relocating elsewhere. This group is regarded as being cosmopolitan.

Culture shock has many different effects, degrees of severity and symptoms. Some migrants are stuck and need assistance to move forward (also refer to Chapter 12). If you want to succeed, just don't get stuck in this stage.

The adaptation stage

As you become more confident in your ability to function in two different cultures, you will develop a sense of belonging and will start to feel part of the community. The adaptation stage is also called the "mastery stage". You are more comfortable in the new country, and you even start calling it "home". You operate more confidently in your new milieu without feeling the anxiety; for example, you don't think where to drive anymore.

This doesn't mean total mastery or fluidity every day, but it is getting better with only several moments of stress.

Culturally appropriate behaviour is now second nature to you, and you can trust your instincts because they have been reconditioned by the new culture. It takes little effort now for you to be culturally sensitive. Most migrants do keep traits from their earlier culture, such as accents and language.

Common problems associated with culture shock are:
1. Information overload (and wrong advice on social media).
2. Language barriers (difficulties in communication experienced by people speaking different languages).
3. Generation gap (difference of opinions between one generation and another regarding beliefs, politics, or values).
4. Homesickness (cultural and linguistic).

5. Boredom (being overly dependent on a job to provide identity and security).
6. Responsibility for cultural changes (your cultural awareness skills set).

There is no magic formula to prevent culture shock, as any individual in any society is affected differently on a personal level by cultural contrasts.

BICULTURAL IDENTITY

Eventually, migrants will develop a bicultural identity. This is the condition of being oneself regarding the combination of two cultures. The term can also be defined as biculturalism, which is the presence of two different cultures in the same country or region. Some examples of biculturalism: African American culture, French Canadian culture, and Polish Australian culture.

Paul Pederson mentioned in his book, *The five stages of culture shock,* that this process is a profoundly personal experience. It doesn't affect all people the same way, or even the same person in the same way when it reoccurs.

Some migrants may find it extremely difficult to assimilate both their cultural contexts. To succeed in developing your bicultural identity, you need to reconcile your current host culture with your culture of origin (native culture).

Human beings are more influenced by the dominant values that they have learned in their native culture. Since the day we are born, we are raised with cultural and social filters which are also known as biases or belief systems. The older we get, the more hardwired and ingrained they become, and the more difficult it is to adapt and change.

A few examples of some of these mainstream cultural and social filters are:
1. Certain jobs, like cleaning and rubbish removal, are for lower-class people.
2. A woman's place is in the kitchen.

3. Only certain ethnic groups can do a proper job.
4. People from other nationalities are not trustworthy.
5. Refugees and asylum seekers from war-torn countries can't adapt to Australian society due to the trauma they suffered.

Many Australians will find it strange that you can't recognise your cultural and social filters or even try to change them.

ACCULTURATION

Acculturation is the process in which a bicultural individual or migrant adopts the social norms of the mainstream society. The cultural gap between migrant parents and their children may widen due to acculturation. Younger generations find it easier to adapt to the new culture, which may strain your family relationship. It can also lead to some very funny moments when your children will correct your pronunciation.

Many migrant parents need to make peace with grandchildren who may not understand their mother-tongue and the possibility of future in-laws being of a different ethnic culture.

However, migrants and bicultural families do have more positive roles to play. They have strong commitments to their families and have dreams of a better life. This, in turns, gives families a sense of purpose and connection and strengthens the family unit. Native customs such as holidays and religious affiliations may also support the family unit and promote unity all around.

We are all different and unique. No two people experience things exactly alike. Oberg's stages provide us with a broad overview of what could be expected within the first two years of living in Australia.

The culture shock phases have three basic outcomes. If you or any family members struggle with the acculturation process, read Chapter 12 on how to take care of yourself and your family.

Note: *An interesting fact is that it is impossible to know everything about a culture, even your own culture. Culture is continually altering and developing.*

REVERSE CULTURE SHOCK

Reverse culture shock is also known as "re-entry shock" or "own culture shock". This takes place when you return to your home country for a visit or holiday.

Mental note to every immigrant reading this chapter – going back to your home country is not a holiday. You usually return feeling more exhausted than energised. If you want to go on a holiday in your home country, book a vacation with only your core family unit and take a complete break from visiting family and friends. Family and friends that stayed behind are still wedged in their established thought patterns (some very negative), living in their own little worlds (emotional numbing or dissociation) and not open to anything new or alien to their ethnic identity.

AUSTRALIAN ECCENTRICITIES

Australians are a weird mob of people until you finally get your head around why they perceive the world the way they do. It is a different culture with many contradicting nuances (social and cultural filters) that are sometimes difficult to understand.

Tall Poppy Syndrome (TPS)

The phrase, "tall poppy syndrome", can be found in written media as early as 1864, but it became more prevalent in Australian society from 1904.

TPS is the unspoken national ethos that no Australian or foreigner is permitted to assume that he or she is better than any other Australian. Australians enforce this national ethos with prompt, corrective or levelling ridicule. The tallest flower (poppy) in the field will be cut down to the same size as all the others. Most of the time, this concept is misunderstood. It isn't the success that offends Australians. It's the offence or insult committed by anyone who starts to put on superior airs. Do you see now why we said you should leave your ego back home?

Many migrants have experienced and observed the cynical, sarcastic, and passive-aggressive behaviour towards themselves and fellow migrants. Migrants have a really hard time with this phenomenon. You are passionate and eager to move forward, inspired, and ready to make a difference, just be told off!

An American blogger, Amy, wrote an article about TPS on her blog, *Things Aussies Like*. Several Australians replied to her article, but the response below best explained the essence of TPS (shortened):

"As an Aussie I can assure you Tall Poppy Syndrome is much more about cutting down the arrogance associated with success, than it is about cutting down genuine success. It's not that we Aussies don't want others to succeed, it's just that we value humility to the point of bringing someone back "down to earth" if their ego starts to inflate. That's not to say we won't allow people to be proud of their achievements; celebration for achievements brought about by hard work is typically accepted. It's when people start bragging, expecting preferential treatment or starting to display an "air" of superiority (which we are apt to sniff out) that we tend to stick a pin in their ballooning ego. We simply LOATHE arrogance."

TPS is alive and well in Australian culture. Rest assured you are not alone. You will eventually figure it out. Always remember: "If you are a tall poppy, keep your head down."

Equality

The basic rules of Australian social etiquette do not relate to how a fork should be held or who should be served first at a dinner table. Instead, most of Australia's rules relate to expressing equality. Basically, if you appreciate that Australians want to be treated as equals, irrespective of their social, racial, or financial background, anything is acceptable.

Furthermore, because Australians see all people as equal, they frequently offend international visitors who feel a more respectful attitude is warranted. A very good example of this was when cricketer Dennis Lillee expressed his egalitarian sentiments when he greeted Queen Elizabeth using the words: "G'day, how ya goin'?"

In Dennis' mind, he was just treating the Queen as an equal. After all, it wasn't her fault that she couldn't play cricket. Nor was she responsible for her subjects being terrible cricket players. But to many English people, Lillee's expression of equality was viewed as the act of a fool.

Australians became an egalitarian society because people who were treated as second class citizens refused to accept that they were in any way inferior. This refusal to accept inferiority greatly differentiates Australia from its neighbours, where hierarchical thinking prevails.

Expressing generosity

Generosity may be a sign of bludging (to impose on) or inferiority and Australians may frown upon the gesture. Australians do not expect birthday gifts or even Christmas gifts, for that matter.

At the workplace, they have a tradition called "Kris Krinkle". It is the same as a secret Santa gift exchange. You pick someone's name out of a hat, and you are responsible for giving that person a gift at the Christmas party. The value of the gift is capped at a maximum of $15 or $20, depending on the general office consensus regarding the value. Do not spend more than the capped amount. You have nothing to prove!

If you have a big, charitable heart, in Australia, it is better to channel it through volunteering and making monthly donations through registered charities. People don't want to be perceived as your "charity case". Money given to charities is also tax-deductible at the end of the financial year.

Socialising

If you think that it is best to keep your distance than to make a social faux pas, think again. When you are reluctant to engage or participate in social events in the workplace, Australians will start distrusting you. It will be perceived as if you think you are better than them or maybe that you have something to hide. Go out and socialise, buy a round of beers and take part in the banter (even if goes straight over your head in the beginning).

Banter

Australians are not easily offended, and therefore they are not sensitive to causing offence in others. To outsiders, Australians often appear very blunt and rude. They tend to call a spade a spade when perhaps more tact is required.

During our preparations to move to Australia, we bought a book: *Culture Shock Australia*. The writer used an analogy which we found very odd at the time, but after living in Australia, it made more sense. He compared Australians' humour or banter to a brick going through a windscreen. A group of Australian men wouldn't think twice to jokingly tell a pregnant colleague that she needs to lose some weight or ask her if she is sure that she is not carrying twins or triplets.

Workplace culture

The relaxed attitude of Australians in some workplaces has been known to cause problems for many migrants. If you come from a workplace culture where tomorrow is *not* another day, close enough is *not* good enough and putting a problematic issue in the too hard basket, hoping it will eventually go away or sort itself out, you may struggle with the Australian workplace culture.

Many migrants have to restrain themselves in the workplace and struggle to get their heads around being more relaxed. Some migrants have an innate urgency to get things done, especially Dutch, German, and South African migrants.

Most Asian cultures are not used to challenging authority, and sometimes the outspoken or loud manager will be overwhelming for the new arrival – it really does take time to get used to a new management style.

If you come from a country where you address your colleagues as "sir" or "mam" the Australian way of addressing your colleagues by their first names or some distorted version of the surname could create major anxiety to a newly arrived migrant worker.

Embrace the more relaxed Australian way, take care of yourself, and maybe you will live longer without having a heart attack or stroke along the way.

The day when you are called "mate" at work, you will know that you have been accepted and are part of the team.

Patriotism

Australians have an odd attitude to patriotism. On the one hand, they can mock their own country in front of an international audience without any real sense of personal shame. It is almost as if they are afraid the international audience will think that Australia is superior in any way, so they need to cut their own country down to avoid being accused of supremacist thinking.

Even though they will be extremely critical of their own country, the same Australians won't champion any foreign culture as being superior to Australia. If any country is held up as being superior to Australia, especially America, they will generally find a reason to argue otherwise or cut the foreign culture down.

The best advice still comes from the 1957 movie; *They're a Weird Mob*:

> *"Learn the Aussie way.*
> *Learn the Aussie language.*
> *Get yourself accepted as one of them;*
> *and you will enter a world that you never dreamed existed.*
> *And once you have entered it, you will never leave it."*

SUMMARY OF RECOMMENDATIONS

1. Do more research and become familiar with the Australian language and customs. Websites to visit:
    -   www.alldownunder.com
    -   www.convictcreations.com
    -   www.australiaday.com.au/get-involved/

2. Ask a neighbour or fellow settled countryman to take you on an orientation walk or tour in the city. Learn how to use and access the public transport system.

3. Find Australian migrants who have been in Australia for some time and have adjusted with a positive attitude. Talk to them about your difficulties.

4. Talk to people who have a positive attitude toward your new host country. Don't be too surprised if friends and family from "back home" have negative things to say about Australia. This is mostly because they miss you or can't really relate to your new life.

5. Build a community around you. Enrol in a class, join a choir or orchestra, card club, or other social groups. Volunteering is the best way to become involved, meet people and get some Australian work experience.

6. Stay in touch with family and friends in your home country. E-mail, Skype and instant messaging make this easy. If you don't have access to a computer, plan to write short letters or postcards to friends and family. If you have children, encourage them to communicate with people back home. Encourage close family members to come and visit after you have settled in (preferably in the first year or two).

7. Balance socializing with fellow countrymen with getting to know the local people. Make an effort to spend time with Australians and your neighbours. This will help you integrate faster. Food is a great way to bring people together. Don't be concerned about the "vegan" guests or special diets, just go for it. You could even prepare some of your traditional food; they will love it.

8. Make your relationship a priority if you are a couple. Actively provide comfort and show concern for each other. Explore the host country together. Figure out how you can work together during the adjustment period. Add "check-in" dates onto your calendar to make time to connect with each other.

9. Set reasonable and realistic goals for yourself but also create family goals. Divide your goals into weekly, monthly and yearly goals. Write them down, make a vision board and put it somewhere accessible to everybody in the family.

   Examples of goals:
   - Learn a few Aussie words every day or week.
   - Meet one of your neighbours.
   - Get your qualifications accredited.
   - Visit local areas of interest.
   - Start saving for a trip back to your home country (in 2-3 years).

10. Give yourself time. You have spent many years learning about your own identity, culture and home country. Do not expect to learn everything about Australia in a few weeks' time.

9

JOBSEEKING AND DOING BUSINESS

"Self-introspection is the way to improve any company, any marriage,
any nation. And any job-hunt."

~ Richard N. Bolles
(In: What Color Is Your Parachute?)

Let's put a few things into perspective first, so you can try to relate to the unemployment rate, job stability and the size of the workforce in Australia.

THE AUSTRALIAN WORKFORCE
Australia's unemployment rate was a mere 4% before the COVID-19 pandemic, less than 1 million people, and the rate has been more or less stable since around 2012. However, new figures from the Federal Government indicate that the unemployment rate may rise to 10% due to the pandemic. For migrants looking for a job, this is not good news at all, but if you follow the tips in this chapter, you will have a good head start.

There are many misconceptions when it comes to doing business in Australia. What most migrants don't realise, is what a melting pot of different cultures Australia is. There are so many different cultures in the workplace: European, British, Asian and Indian. The City of Melbourne states that 56% of its residents were born overseas!

If you are used to certain stereotypes, please forget any of them. All these cultures blend well in one space. You are about to join a very multicultural workplace, and it is an excessively big country.

Keep in mind, however, that you will still be working in a predominantly Australian workforce. You should dismiss any preconceived ideas you have about Australians as being loud, rude, and maybe even lazy or childish. As with any culture, you need to understand the root of the behaviour and learn to accept, adapt, and embrace it.

Remember that for the first 100 years of white settlements in Australia, convicts were brought in by boat by the thousands. Most of these convicts were only accused of petty crimes. They were poorly educated, and only 20% were female. Inevitably the society that started growing here was male-dominated, with much drinking, gambling and brawling taking place.

You can imagine 80% of the population consisting of convicts, with 20% trying to maintain law and order. These early settlers set the trend for Australians to question authority, to challenge unfair demands, and to bond together in "mateship".

With job security and the combination of tall poppy syndrome, as discussed in Chapter 8, everybody does his or her bit and gets on with the job at hand.

Many migrants are used to wearing "multiple hats" in their line of work and doing the work of more than one person. In Australia, on the other hand, employees have very defined roles. This creates a lot of tension and anxiety for migrants. They feel that they have a magnitude of different skills and can do so much more!

Perhaps this is one of the reasons why migrants perceive Australians as lazy. To them, results are important, but sometimes the detailed planning will be sacrificed to get things done. There usually are no meetings to interpret further, analyse or predict the outcomes. Rather, it is a team environment where each has his or her part to play, and they focus on the bigger picture, not the infinite detail.

If you try to jump ahead and do the work of ten people, you will be cut down very quickly (Tall Poppy Syndrome). This can be difficult for migrants, as they can be used to working hard and fighting for a career, job security and status, none of which are high priorities for Australians.

Remember, as a new arrival; you are suffering a loss of identity. You desperately want to have the same respect you had back in your home country. You want people to understand how hard you can work and that you were really liked around the office.

This will happen in due time. In the meantime, try to relax a little. You want to prove yourself, we get that, we've been there, but it is not going to happen overnight. Australians will do business with you if they like *you*, not your assets or performance. Be humble, be present, engage with them, and show them that you are a team player.

FIRST MEETINGS OR INTERVIEWS

Although Aussies don't necessarily judge you, we do believe in making a good first impression. To be on the safe side, always dress up for the first occasion. Wear a suit or appropriate clothing. If you are wearing a suit, only remove your jacket if invited to do so. In some situations, it is not rude to ask if there is a dress code.

Don't wait to be introduced, especially if you are part of a group. Feel free to put out your hand and say: "Hi, I am ..." First names are usually preferred and perfectly okay. If it makes you feel more comfortable, you can check with the person. If you address someone as "Mr" or "Mrs Surname", it will be so out of character in Australia that they will quickly correct you and say: "Just call me Bob."

Generally, an interview or first meeting will start with some social chitchat to get to know each other, so don't dive straight into business. Some migrants can be very direct and to the point, just like the Australians, but there is a time and place for it. The Australians do like an honest, straight talker, but their timing is a little different.

In some cultures, people jump straight in to gain the respect of those around the table as soon as possible. In Australia, people get to know each other first, because you are not being judged on how well you chair a meeting. If you are meeting for a coffee, which is most usual, then the cue to start business talk is generally once the coffee arrives. We use this approximate timing in any situation.

Australians are usually used to multicultural dealings but on a very superficial level. They are genuinely interested in cultures but expect that you will bridge the gap between their culture and your own.

Without talking too much about yourself, feel free to explain yourself or your culture to help them build a picture of you. This should not be a cue to spill out your life story. A typical Australian will switch off very quickly if you start sharing personal issues. You could, however, explain that you are used to working in a fast-paced environment, so you are used to getting involved in all aspects of the job.

Don't try to be a know-it-all – remember what we've said about tall poppy syndrome. Australians prefer your questions to your string of facts. They believe it was a bad day if they didn't have a good laugh, so always try to end with something that you both enjoyed about the meeting or something you can look forward to at your next meeting.

APPLYING FOR JOBS

If you have not been fortunate enough to land a job before arriving, then brace yourself for many cups of coffee to make new acquaintances, or, as our cultural coach, Patti McCarthy says, "kiss a lot of frogs".

If you have decided not to associate with other migrants from your home country, then you are making a big mistake when it comes to job searches. Your fellow countrymen know what you are going through, they can relate to that, and they might have contacts who might be able to help you if they can't. Fellow countrymen will help you much sooner than anyone else, if possible.

THE FIRST STEPS TO TAKE IN FINDING A JOB

Create a professional network
If you are not on the **LinkedIn** platform, then get on it straight away (www.linkedin.com). It is widely used across Australia. You can do this well in advance before you move to Australia. Update your profile and make sure you have a professional business profile picture, not one with the biggest fish you ever caught, or your fur baby!

Have a clear, polished LinkedIn profile, keeping it concise and easy to read. It should be a "taster" of your CV (more commonly known in Australia as a résumé). If someone is reading your profile online, you will not hold their attention for very long, so keep it simple and effective.

Top tip: *Make sure that you have a professional email address. Email addresses like han_solo@starwars.com are not perceived as professional.*

Groups
Once your LinkedIn profile looks professional, start joining groups in your industry. This way, you can connect with others in the same field, and eventually reach out to them for potential positions in their company.
Make sure you are making comments on discussions posted in the group, and if relevant, connect with the person who commenced the discussion.

You might also want to join a LinkedIn group, which is also a good space where you can connect with fellow countrymen who are already settled in Australia. There are various groups in each city, and most of them meet up at least once a month.

Companies
Follow companies that interest you or are within your industry. If you have been invited for an interview, LinkedIn can provide very up to date information on that company. Any news articles and company announcements are published on LinkedIn much quicker than on a company website.

Endorsements and recommendations
Ask your colleagues and friends from your home country to endorse your LinkedIn-profile and give you recommendations. Remember to bring any referral letters, recommendations, and qualifications with you when you come to Australia.

Employment websites
Some useful employment websites are:
1. www.bluecollar.com.au (blue-collar jobs only)
2. www.jobnet.com.au (recruitment site for IT jobs)
3. www.careerone.com.au
4. www.seek.com.au
5. www.indeed.com
6. www.ethicaljobs.com.au (not-for-profit and community jobs)
7. www.probonoaustralia.com.au (not-for-profit and community jobs)

Qualifications formally recognised
It is advisable to have your qualifications formally recognised by the relevant authority in Australia. This may improve your chance of gaining employment in your profession or trade.

If you have trade qualifications in areas such as engineering, construction, metalwork, electrical work or catering, **Trades Recognition Australia**, can advise you on how to have those qualifications recognised in Australia: (www.tradesrecognitionaustralia.gov.au)

If you are looking for work in a specific occupation, you

should contact the registration, licensing or professional body listed on the Australian Skills Recognition Information website to check whether your qualifications are recognised in Australia.

If you have tertiary qualifications and you want to use them in Australia, you can contact a state or territory government **Overseas Qualification Unit** (OQU), and they can assess how your qualification compares to an Australian qualification using the Australian Qualification Framework. This service is free. The Department of Education, Employment and Workplace Relations (DEEWR) through Australian Education International – National Office of Overseas Skills Recognition (**AEI-NOOSR**) provides general information and advice on the comparison of overseas qualifications. Check with the overseas qualification unit in your state or territory before contacting AEI-NOOSR. They will refer you to AEI-NOOSR if required https://internationaleducation.gov.au/services-and-resources/pages/qualifications-recognition.aspx

In some cases, overseas-trained professionals holding Australian citizenship or permanent residence may be eligible for **assistance to pay** part or all of their tuition fees (FEE-HELP) for bridging studies required for recognition of prior learning in Australia (www.studyassist.gov.au/help-loans/fee-help). The Assessment Subsidy for Overseas Trained Professionals Program (**ASDOT**) assists financially disadvantaged, overseas trained professionals. If you are eligible, the program provides financial support to cover the cost of assessments and examinations that must be passed to qualify for employment in certain professions in Australia.

YOUR RÉSUMÉ/CV

Once you have a great looking LinkedIn profile, then you should polish up your résumé/CV and make sure there is a link to it on LinkedIn profile. There are thousands of templates on Google, and we recommend that your résumé/CV should fit the look of your industry.

Here are some tips for the best-looking résumé/CV for your industry:

1. Get someone local to **proofread**. Migrants tend to use many words in one sentence, trying to explain themselves clearly and saying the same thing in a few different ways to be understood. This can be very distracting for an Australian reader. Find an Australian who can proofread your CV or visit www.pillarsofpower.com.au for a professional to assist with your CV.

2. Most **Australian résumés/CV** have:
    *   **Personal information:** Your name and contact details at the top of the page.
    *   **Professional profile:** 4 to 8 line introduction about your experience and ambitions.
    *   **Key skills:** Bullet points of your key skills over the duration of your career.
    *   **Professional experience:** Job title, employment dates, key responsibilities and achievements in bullet form.
    *   **Your education and further studies**, along with any further contact information or references.

Remember:
Australians like a team player, not an individual with a big ego. Try to avoid using the word "I" too many times in your résumé. Replace "I" with "we" where possible. Instead of saying: "I improved productivity by 30%", rather say: "Our team improved productivity by 30%."

What **not to put** on your résumé/CV:
1. Your date of birth.
2. Your gender.
3. Your religious affiliation.
4. Your secondary school name and results.
5. Your home country's military service or experience.

RECRUITERS

As with anywhere else around the globe, there are recruiters working in specific industries or on behalf of specific companies. Many job applications can be made online, but don't be afraid to walk into offices or shops with your résumé and hand it in or complete an application form.

Just like with estate agents, you won't get much engagement until you are actually in Australia, but don't let that stop you from trying. There is much fish in the sea, and you might just strike it lucky.

Once you have a polished LinkedIn profile and sparkling résumé, it is time to hit the streets and start "kissing frogs". Contact recruitment agencies – there are a few great ones out there, just make sure they are working in your industry.

Talk to as many people as you can and try to stay positive. People will always help someone much faster if the person is positive. Try not to let it all get you down, even if it is hard. If you are having a bad day, then be the one asking the questions. Ask about their weekend, their kids, where they live.

Be interested in the other person to deflect them from asking you too much, especially when you are not in a positive frame of mind.

Take a few deep breaths: it is not easy, but you are employable, and you can add value to any organisation, you just need to find the right one – fast.

Hang in there and remember to connect with your fellow countrymen where you can relax a little and let your hair down. Feel comfortable that someone else "gets you". Keep smiling; you will get there.

VOLUNTEERING

Volunteering is the Australian way of life. Just about everybody we know volunteers their time and expertise somewhere or somehow. This is a great way to gain experience, learn about local culture and work ethic, and it is highly regarded on your résumé. Volunteering will build your self-esteem, and the valuable experience on your résumé is immeasurable!

Volunteer opportunities can be found on:
1. **Volunteer** (www.volunteer.com.au)
2. **Go volunteer** (www.govolunteer.com.au)

Many organisations across industries provide volunteering opportunities. Make sure to search for your relevant industry.

Positive outcomes from volunteering:

1. Any volunteering will boost your credibility in Australia.

2. You gain valuable knowledge about Australian Health and Safety regulations.

3. Even if you volunteer only one day per week, you will have Australian references for your résumé.

4. It shows employers that you are willing to integrate.

5. Many volunteer positions eventually become full-time positions.

6. If you work with children, you need to have an official "Working with children" check done. As a volunteer, there is no charge for this check.

7. Volunteering helps with integration and meeting new people.

8. Volunteering is the best, most natural antidepressant.

RECOGNITION OF PRIOR LEARNING

In Australia, there are many pathways to get your qualifications and skills certified. They don't look at you as an empty slate with foreign qualifications. In fact, they look at you as a whole person who has many skills, experiences and expertise.

The only thing that they do want is to have everybody on the same playing fields to give everybody a "fair go".

The recognition of prior learning approach acknowledges that people may have gained appropriate knowledge, understanding, and skills during their previous work, volunteering, travelling or personal experience.

This experience could be from paid and unpaid work.

Examples of unpaid work are:
1. School class co-ordinator at your children's school.
2. Bookkeeping for your husband's business.
3. Chairperson of a community-based organisation's council/board.
4. Organising fundraising events at your children's school.
5. Freelance traveller blog writing.

Depending on what Australian qualification you want to RPL all the above-mentioned experiences, skills and competencies could be considered. They also take into consideration any competencies you as an individual developed as a result of engaging in learning experiences in Australia or your home country.

1. Someone who has spent many years working as a PA within an office setting will have developed many skills that are part of a qualification in business administration.

2. Previous work experience in an automotive/mechanic workshop may have provided someone with competencies that are relevant to a qualification in mechanics.

3. If you have spent time helping out at a tuition centre for underprivileged children, you may have some experience that is relevant to a teaching certification. The same scenario goes for aged care and disability care.

4. Maybe you are a seasoned bookkeeper and has tried many times to finish your Accounting Degree part-time, but life and finances keep on getting in the way.

It could happen that previous work, voluntary and learning experiences may not be enough to provide you with full recognition of prior learning. However, the competencies that you have gained can be used as credit towards units of competency. This may result in reducing the amount of time or the number of modules you need to require completing a qualification, which saves you money.

Recognised Training Organisations (RTOs) take the following into consideration:

1. an individual's existing skills and knowledge as acquired in a practical, non-formal or formal learning setting, and

2. assessing whether that person can demonstrate the required competencies associated with the relevant Australian standards.

A good example of this scenario is when you have loads of bookkeeping experience, but you haven't used the MYOB software program that is required for a bookkeeping certificate or diploma. You will then receive RPL or credit for some of the required units for the qualification. When you have completed some units, you will receive the full, recognised Australian qualification.

Who can apply for the RPL process?

Anyone who has previous knowledge, experience, or skills that are relevant to the course of study that they want to complete, can apply for this process, regardless of whether your training or experience was in Australia or your home country.

To be successful, you need to be able to provide evidence of the skills and knowledge you have gained. You will undergo an interview to assess your goals and help you choose the right qualification that matches your skills.

Evidence portfolio:
Gather evidence (not older than two years) such as:
1. Current résumé.
2. Current position description detailing your responsibilities.
3. Reference letters.
4. Employment-related examples/samples.
5. Photos/videos.
6. Certificates and transcripts of overseas qualifications.

Skills check:
Once the assessors have gone through your portfolio, they will call you in for a competency conversation and a practical observation, if required.

Qualifications:
All certificates are nationally recognised and issued by a recognised training organisation.

Top tips:

1. *Think ahead while you are still in your home country. Look at the Department of Education and Training (DET)'s website to investigate all the current training packages that are available. You may want to do something completely different, like caring for the aged – this could be the opportunity you have been waiting for your whole life.*

2. *Volunteer while you have the opportunity and gather any evidence you may possibly need before you leave for Australia.*

3. *Pack your evidence in a carton box that is easily identifiable for easy access when needed.*

4. *Don't think that you are above a TAFE qualification. With all your degrees and diplomas (which are recognised by Australia), you could still struggle to find a job in your current specialist field.*

5. *Contact us at www.pillarsofpower.com.au for an initial assessment and advice sooner, rather than later. It is easier to build your evidence portfolio and gather information and examples while you are still in your home country.*

Job advertisements will usually state something like:
"For an applicant to be successful in obtaining this position, the applicant needs to have:
1. *At least 5-10 years of experience working with Aboriginal and Torres Islander clients or 5 years' experience working in the vocational education sector.*
2. *Demonstrated experience or extensive experience in...*

3. Working knowledge of system ABC and XYZ government reporting portal."

The first requirement for the position mentioned above already makes migrants fall entirely out of the bus. Sometimes you must go down on the job ladder before you can go up again. We all have work experience and skills that are transferable to other sectors and industries. Be flexible, be open-minded and go for it!

STARTING A BUSINESS

Moving to another country is a great time to start over, try something new, and in the traditional Aussie-style, give it a go!

We might be generalising when we say migrants often don't tend to have an entrepreneurial mindset. Migrants are strong-willed people who are eager to learn. Yet, we find that the thought of "going solo" and starting your own company is sometimes too daunting and worrisome for most migrants.

Many migrants are brought up to find a good stable job, not really to fly off the edge of a cliff into your own business. When you arrive in a new country, the security a job provides also takes the pressure off. But now you are in Australia.

For the fourth year in a row, business start-ups have increased by more than 4% across the country. Most of this growth is seen in small businesses which are sole entrepreneurs.

The process of opening a business is straightforward, even if you have just arrived. It is easy to navigate websites, and webinars and podcasts are at your fingertips.

Most local councils host at least three information evenings or webinars per month. Many of these cost under $20, and they could include sessions on tax, social media marketing, improving profit and many more.

The cost to start a business will depend on the type of business structure and turnover. The application for an Australian Business Number (ABN) is made online, and you will need your Tax Number (TFN) to proceed.

All your answers can be found on the easy to navigate website: www.business.gov.au

For further information on opening a business:
www.ausmumpreneur.com
https://blog.hubspot.com/marketing/how-to-start-a-business-in-australia

Apply for your Australian business number:
www.ato.gov.au/Business/International-tax-for-business/Foreign-residents-doing-business-in-Australia/Australian-business-number-(ABN)/

Real-life story

We found that with most of the migrants we relocate, at least one spouse has a job already lined up. The other spouse often starts his or her own company. Many migrants offer work as virtual assistants, personal trainers, make-up artists, hairdressers, jewellery and interior designers, photographers, and the list goes on.

One of the most heart-warming stories was a young lady who had followed her husband to Melbourne. They were newlyweds and very positive and excited. She had held a marketing job in their home country but had this intense desire to work with flowers.

Within just a few weeks of arriving, she opened a little business that held workshops in floral arrangements. It was an instant hit with companies for team building sessions; with girls getting together for maybe a hens' night or even a book club evening.

The best part was that her workshops extended to the cancer ward in Monash hospital. Her love of flowers was bringing joy to so many others.

SUMMARY OF RECOMMENDATIONS

1. Do research and become familiar with the Australian job market.

2. Contact us at www.pillarsofpower.com.au for an initial assessment and advice sooner rather than later for assistance with recognition of prior learning. It is easier to build your evidence portfolio while you are still in your home country.

3. Buy our book, *Your D.I.Y. Australian Job-hunting Guide*, for more extensive information, links, templates, and advice on:
   - Résumés,
   - Cover letters
   - Qualifications
   - Australian experience
   - Networking
   - Social media profiles
   - Interviewing skills
   - Working in a multicultural workplace

10

RULES, RULES AND MORE RULES!

"For to be free is not merely to cast off one's chains,
But to live in a way that respects and enhances the freedom of others."

~ *Nelson Mandela (Political leader and philanthropist)*

Many migrants emigrate from their home countries because they want law and order in their lives. They yearn to experience for religious freedom or maybe justice where perpetrators are caught and punished for their crimes.

However, many migrants arrive in Australia and are absolutely abhorred with all the rules and regulations. They complain, resist and even challenge the Australian way of running their society, communities and workplaces. They try to cut corners and get things done in their usual, no-nonsense way.

In this chapter, we are introducing you to some of the rules that will not only affect you in the workplace but also in everyday life situations, from electrical issues around the home to school parties and even volunteering at your place of worship.

WHAT IS WORK/OCCUPATIONAL HEALTH AND SAFETY (W/OHS)?

We found that migrants "push back" because they don't understand the reasons for the implementation of all the rules and regulations.

Some migrants, like the French or South Africans who dislike bureaucracy, are used to making plans, whether for their own safety or just to get by. They will try to find a way around almost everything!

Needless to say, many migrants are a very resourceful and innovative bunch of people who find personal satisfaction in finding solutions.

In Australia, you can't do anything without putting up a safety warning sign, put on a bright-orange bib or applying for a licence. By cutting corners in Australia, you are not only making life difficult for yourself, but you may also put yourself and other people at risk.

If you apply for a job, knowledge about the legislation is required, and you have to be prepared to answer questions about it during interviews.

Of course, these rules and regulations are not unique to Australia. If you emigrate to the USA, Canada, New Zealand, the United Kingdom or any other first world country, for that matter, you will be confronted with a new set of rules, regulations and legislation.

WHS is the proverbial thorn in most migrants' flesh. However, in the instance where you are the injured victim, this knowledge could be helpful to receive financial support in a situation that would have otherwise been devastating.

According to the Australian Workers' Compensation Statistics report:

1. Work-related injuries such as injury and musculoskeletal disorders led to 90% of serious claims in 2014-2015.
2. The most common injuries were traumatic joint/ligament and muscle/tendon injuries (almost 45%).
3. In work-related situations, diseases led to 10% of serious claims.

THE IMPORTANCE OF WORK/OCCUPATIONAL HEALTH AND SAFETY

WHS is concerned with protecting the safety, health and welfare of people engaged in work or employment. The enjoyment of these standards at the highest levels is a fundamental human right that should be accessible by each and every worker.

Regardless of the nature of their work, workers should be able to carry out their responsibilities in a safe and secure working environment, free from hazards. These rights are set out in legislation to ensure that employers are clear about the obligations and the consequences for neglecting them.

You may think that this only relates to the mining, construction and manufacturing industries. However, it relates to all work or employment in Australia. It also includes mental health issues at workplaces such as burnout, compassion fatigue, stress, bullying and sexual harassment. Workplace injury or disease has the ability to destroy your quality of life, social and family activities, job prospects and future career advancement.

According to the Australian Council of Trade Unions, a worker is seriously injured every 2-3 minutes. In 2017, 190 workers were fatally injured while at work and 106 260 serious claims were received, with a median of $11,500 per claim in workers' compensation.

Workplace injuries, diseases and fatalities, in the 2018 financial year, were estimated to around $61.8 billion in foregone economic activity, or 4.8% of Australia's total GDP. These rules and regulations are implemented by workplaces to protect themselves from WorkCover claims but also to protect employees (from themselves in some cases!).

NON-COMPLIANCE TO W/OHS REGULATIONS

Work Health and Safety laws (WHS) are based on national model legislation that is now enforced in all Australian states and territories, except Victoria and Western Australia, where earlier Occupational Health and Safety laws (OHS) still apply.

These laws aim to protect people's health and safety at work by imposing obligations on all parties who are in a position to contribute to the successful management of workplace risks. This applies to manufacturers and suppliers of equipment and substances, as well as employers, workers, contractors, and others.

In each jurisdiction, an Act of Parliament supported by regulations is administered by the relevant WHS or OHS regulator – generally known as WorkCover or WorkSafe. The regulator provides advice and guidance and enforces the law through its inspectorate.

WHS laws are supported by codes of practice that provide practical guidance in achieving the standards of health and safety required by law. Model WHS codes of practice are also developed at the national level and subsequently adopted by the various state and territory authorities, where harmonised WHS laws have been implemented.

The **protection of children and vulnerable people** are taken even more seriously. Under the Working with Children Act 2005 (the Act), only people who are doing child-related work and who are not exempt need a check. This applies to both paid and volunteer workers.

The Working with Children Check (WWCC) also accompanies a recent police check (less than one-month-old). In most other countries, anybody can teach Sunday school at church or assist with activities where children are involved. In Australia, you need to have a Working with Children Check, current police check and preferably child-safe training.

If you apply for teaching or childcare positions, you will also need:
1. A current approved first aid qualification.
2. A current approved anaphylaxis management training.
3. A current approved emergency asthma management training.

So many migrants get upset and irritated with all these rules and regulations, but it is there to protect you (the parent/employee), the children you are working with and also your own children.

You don't want to be responsible for a child's death due to a peanut allergy because you didn't know how to assist the child. Or even worse, be investigated for child abuse because you didn't know what the legal engagement parameters are in Australia.

The above-mentioned training needs and checks should be renewed and updated regularly, depending on the specific state-based legislation. This is taken very seriously by organisations, and I've worked in organisations where people lost their jobs due to non-compliance with the policies and legislation.

W/OHS REGULATIONS IN EVERYDAY LIFE

Most organisations or companies will have a dedicated Risk Management Department or at least a WHS manager. Many migrants look at WHS and think that it is common sense.

Feedback about WHS from migrants are:
"Why can't people look where they are going?"
"You can't blame everybody else for your own stupidity."
"Looks like common sense is not so common anymore."

Even though these are valid arguments, there is always that one person who you need to cater for who don't have common sense. Maybe the person has new glasses with multifocal lenses and still needs to get used to them. Or a colleague partied too hard over the weekend and is still a bit unstable on his feet on Monday morning. The employer *must* ensure a safe work environment for everybody.

A psychological WHS issue that is very prominent and newsworthy lately in Australia is the physical and emotional abuse of ambulance workers and emergency room hospital staff.

The psychological effect on a person's mental health is not always immediately visible and can have far-reaching consequences if not pro-actively managed.

Supermarkets/bakeries/food shops
1. Bread dough for pizzas:
   Against OHS regulations. They can't control the conditions the food was kept in after it left the supermarket.
2. Perishable food not sold by the end of the day: Destroyed or provided to charities such as Second Bite.
3. Australia doesn't have home industries. Food safety standards place obligations on food businesses to produce food that is safe and suitable to eat.

Food safety standards place obligations of food businesses to produce food that is safe and suitable to eat. Health and hygiene obligations are also placed on food handlers. Even a cake decorator will have her kitchen approved, and the local council will inspect it every year for compliance.

Restaurants
Most restaurants don't provide "doggy bags" for leftover food.

Buses
The bus can't stop randomly at your request. They are only allowed to stop at designated bus stops.

Tram stops
When the tram stops in front of you, you must stop too, to allow passengers to embark or disembark safely.

Children's car seats
Car seats for children must be fitted correctly, must be adjusted for their age and size and must meet Australian Standards (AS 1754).

Children under six months:
Rear-facing child restraints with an inbuilt harness. They may not sit in the front seat.

Children aged six months to under four years:
Rear-facing or forward-facing child restraint with an inbuilt harness. They may not sit in the front seat.

Children aged four years to seven years:
Forward-facing approved child restraint with an inbuilt harness or an approved booster seat with a properly fastened and adjusted seatbelt or child safety harness. They can sit in the front row only if all other rear seats are occupied by children under seven years, in vehicles with two or more rows of seats.

Children aged seven years and older:
A properly adjusted and fastened child restraint or adult seatbelt, depending on the size of the child.

Children seven years and older:
Many children aren't big enough to safely wear an adult seatbelt until they're 10-12 years old. This is because adult seatbelts are designed for people who are at least 145 cm tall.

Nobody is allowed to sit or stand on the back of a ute (Utility vehicle/pick-up). It is illegal in Australia.

Smoking in a vehicle
When children under 16 years of age are present in a vehicle, neither the driver nor any of the passengers are allowed to smoke, whether the vehicle is moving or stationary. Police officers and tobacco control officers have authority to enforce the law by issuing an expiation fee of $75. The maximum penalty is $200. Smoking is also prohibited in work vehicles, which are considered to be enclosed workspaces.

More passengers than seatbelts

You are not allowed to have more passengers in the car than the number of seatbelts fitted. All passengers must wear seatbelts.

Most people in Australia reverse park their vehicles in driveways and carparks because it is easier to check if there are children or people in front of you than behind your car.

Stationery emergency vehicles with flashing lights

Not allowed to drive past an emergency vehicle more than 40 km/h (states have different legislation).

Car keys

It is illegal to leave your car keys inside an unattended vehicle.

Use of mobile phones

You are not allowed to handle your phone while driving. You may only make or take a call when you have a hands-free kit.

Sun safety and general health

Between September to the end of April between 10am and 3pm, provide children with SPF 30 or higher sunscreen, a hat, and sunglasses.

Immunisation schedule (NIP schedule)

Children whose National Immunisation Program (NIP) schedule (www.health.gov.au/health-topics/immunisation) is not up to date are not allowed to attend school, family day-care or other community activities or be transported in an ambulance. Under the current COVID-19 pandemic regulations, the rules on immunisation have tightened.

Before a child can commence school, they need to produce a certificate from the Australian Immunisation Register (AIR). This certificate can take anything from two to six weeks to obtain in some areas. Attend to your child's immunisation sooner rather than later so that you can receive the certificate in time for them to commence school.

For more information visit:
www.servicesaustralia.gov.au/individuals/services/medicar
e/australian-immunisation-register

Buying cigarettes, alcohol, and condoms
Children under the age of 18 years old are not allowed to buy
or be in possession of cigarettes, alcohol, or condoms.

Smoking
1. Smoking is illegal for persons under 18 years of age.
2. You must be older than 18 years to sell cigarettes.
3. You may not smoke in enclosed spaces. This includes
   restaurants, shopping centres, hospitals, workspaces, clubs,
   pubs, airports, train stations or any shared indoor spaces.

   No smoking in outdoor areas such as:
   - public transport,
   - taxi ranks,
   - train platforms,
   - within the swimming flag areas on a beach,
   - within four metres of a public building,
   - within cultural buildings,
   - cultural heritage venues,
   - near traffic lights,
   - pedestrian crossings, and
   - children's sport or play areas, varying from four
     metres to ten metres according to state regulations.

4. You may only smoke at alfresco dining areas if there is a
   designated smoking area, and the establishment carries a
   liquor licence.
5. Cigarette advertising is banned.
6. Cigarettes should be in enclosed cabinets and not on
   display.
7. Packages should be plain in colour and have sufficient
   health warnings.

8. Fines for smoking in banned areas start at $300 and can exceed $800 in some states.

Prescriptions
The pharmacist will explain all dosages to you even though your GP may have done so already.

Children
Smacking a child is not illegal yet, but very much frowned upon by Australians.

When taking photos of other children at school events, always ask first and make sure what the school's policies are regarding this. Always ask permission before any photos are shared on social media.

Parties at school
Always provide a list of ingredients. Most school policies do not allow food that can cause allergic reactions, such as nuts.

Home
Smoke alarms should be tested regularly. If you are renting, you are responsible for replacing the battery in your smoke alarm.

Fire escape plan for your home/apartment
Everybody should implement a fire escape plan and exercise it regularly.

BBQ safety
Always check the gas connection before you have a BBQ.

Bush and grassfires
If you live in a high-risk area, you should have an evacuation plan.

Total fire bans
No campfires, fires for warmth or personal comfort are allowed.

Light bulb changing

In Victoria, only licensed electricians may change a light bulb. However, it seems that most people are willing to risk the $10 fine and do it themselves.

Pets

Rental properties:
Under the new Residential Tenancies Act, all tenants are allowed to have a pet. That does not mean the landlord might view your application less favourably than someone else without a pet.

The number of pets:
Some councils have restrictions on the number of pets that you may have. You may need a permit for more than two pets.

Registration:
All dogs and cats must be registered with your local council, and you must renew registration every year. Once registered, you will receive a tag. If your pet is found without the tag, you may be fined.

Micro-chipping:
Most councils will not register your dog or cat if it is not micro-chipped and most councils require pets to be desexed. The new microchip must be registered with Central Animal Records (CAR).

The CAR is a free community service run by "The Lost Dogs Home and Cat Shelter". Their aim is to reunite you and your pet if they get lost. You can phone the toll-free number quoting your NPR code, and they can search all the databases to see if your pet is at any pound.

Likewise, if a pound has your animal, your contact details are on file for them to call you. The website is www.car.com.au

Cat curfews:
Legally your cat may not persistently wander onto your neighbours' or other people's property without permission. Most councils set a curfew requiring your cat to be on your property at a set time. The reason for this is to protect native bird and wildlife. Cat-proof fencing and enclosures are very common in Australia.

Dogs:
Your dog must, unless it is exempt from this requirement (assistance dogs), be under the effective control of a competent person at all times when out in public.

This means that it must be on a leash and under the control of someone capable of restraining it.

There are restrictions in Australia of certain breeds of dogs which may not be imported to Australia, such as Pit bulls and some Mastiff breeds.

At the office

Fire drills:
Are done regularly, and all employees participate in these drills. Companies and organisations provide training to designated employees who are responsible for fire safety at the workplace.

First aid:
Most companies and organisations have First Aid Officers that are trained to assist with any emergency.

Electronic equipment:
All portable electronic equipment must be tested and tagged (electrical certification).

OTHER APPLICABLE LEGISLATION

The Charter of Human Rights and Responsibilities (the Charter) comes from a long tradition of international human rights law. At the federal level, the Australian government has an obligation under international law to respect, protect and fulfil human rights. This means the government is obliged to take action to ensure people can enjoy their human rights. The government must also refrain from action that would breach people's human rights.

On a state level, Victoria has taken the lead with their twenty fundamental human rights that are protected in the Charter. The Victorian parliament recognises that, as human beings, we have basic rights, including the right to be treated equally, to be safe from violence and abuse, to be part of a family and to have our privacy respected.

The Victorian Charter of Human Rights and Responsibilities contains twenty basic rights that promote and protect the values of freedom, respect, equality, and dignity.

The Charter sets out the basic rights and freedom of all people in the state. It aims to foster a fairer, more inclusive community by requiring the Victorian government, local councils, and other public authorities to specifically consider human rights when they make laws, develop policies, and provide services.

The Privacy Act 1988 (Privacy Act) regulates the way individuals' personal information is handled.

The Privacy Act allows you to:
1. Know why your personal information is being collected, how it will be used and who it will be disclosed to when needed.
2. Have the option of not identifying yourself, or of using a pseudonym in certain circumstances.
3. Ask for access to your personal information (including your health information).

4. Stop receiving unwanted direct marketing.
5. Ask for your personal information that is incorrect to be corrected.
6. Make a complaint about an entity covered by the Privacy Act, if you consider that they have mishandled your personal information.

WHS regulations not only exist to annoy migrants. They are there to protect your human rights, health, and well-being. After a slip or fall in a public place or at work, make sure that you report the incident according to the relevant policies and procedures. Also, visit your GP and get a referral for X-rays to make sure that there are no hidden injuries that could aggravate over time.

If you feel that your boss or a colleague is bullying or (sexually) harassing you, make sure that you find out exactly what to do, who to contact and where to get support.

Write every incident down, take screenshots of text messages and gather any other relevant paper-based evidence.

When you confront or interact with the colleague, make sure that you have witnesses. Write the date, time, interaction, and the names of the witnesses down in your journal. These notes are important.

The same advice applies to employers who exploit workers by pushing them to the brink of burnout.

In Australia, rules are there to be adhered to, not broken. The lines of communication are very clear, as well as the rules and regulations. There are very few grey areas, and corruption is not common.

Below are organisations that could be contacted if you have any workplace issues:

1. The **Fair Work Commission**, until 2013 known as Fair Work Australia, is the Australian industrial relations tribunal created by the Fair Work Act 2009 (www.fwc.gov.au).

2. The **Australian Human Rights Commission** is a national human rights institution, established in 1986 as the Human Rights and Equal Opportunity Commission and renamed in 2008. It is a statutory body funded by but operating independently of the Australian Government.
Contact them when you have any issues at work regarding sexual harassment or when your disability, age, race, sexual orientation or religious rights are being ignored at the workplace (www.humanrights.gov.au).

3. The **Migrant Workers Centre in Victoria**, for example, empowers migrant workers to understand their rights, enforce them in Victorian workplaces, and connect migrant workers with each other.
(www.migrantworkers.org.au).

Real-life story

Hanna had three falls over a period of eight months due to slippery surfaces (one at a doctor's surgery and two more in a parking area at work). She always felt better after a day or two, took painkillers and soldiered on as she was used to doing in her home country.

Eventually, her ankle broke due to a steady deterioration as a result of the previous injuries. The incident happened at home, and because she never thought about her accidents from a WHS mindset, she had no prior evidence or official report. She had to carry the financial burden for the three subsequent surgeries, ongoing rehabilitation and unpaid sick leave.

SUMMARY OF RECOMMENDATIONS

1. Don't be upset, become aggressive or complain about WHS regulations that you have to adhere to on a daily basis. Just do it!

2. Don't be upset, become aggressive or complain about WHS regulations that you have to adhere to on a daily basis. Just do it!

3. Do your research about WHS regulations in your state and start thinking from a WHS mindset.

4. Know your rights as an employee. If in a management role, know your rights as the employer and effective ways to manage low-performance or unacceptable behaviour in the workplace.

5. When feeling that you are being bullied, abused, or harassed, start writing everything down and gather evidence.

6. Human Resource departments exist to serve the interests of the employer. If you have a workplace issue and you have pursued all the official channels and procedures and still don't have a solution, it is highly recommended that you seek legal advice.

11

NON-ENGLISH SPEAKING MIGRANTS

"Unless you're willing to have a go, fail miserably, and have another go, success won't happen."

~ Phillip Adams
(Australian journalist)

You may ask any non-English speaking migrant, and they will be able to provide you with many humorous and sometimes very embarrassing stories while trying to communicate in English.

To make it just a little bit harder here in Australia, you will also be confronted with Australian slang or "Straya" as the Aussies pronounce it.

Making a complete idiot of yourself due to your grasp of English vocabulary, grammar, pronunciation, or accent is easy. I call this a "migrant moment", the Australians call it a "faux pas". These can vary from hilarious moments to excruciating humiliation, which takes effort and time to process.

NAMES, SURNAMES, NUMBERS, AND TIME

In the **pronunciation** of some names or surnames can be a constant reminder and source of laughter of the challenges most English-speaking people face with foreign names and surnames. Your name and or your surname could become a thorny issue when you emigrate from your home country.

While living in France, my name, Hendrika, was pronounced as "Enric", "Enrica" and even "Enri". The French don't pronounce the "H" sound at the beginning of a name. Our surname changed from Jooste to "Juice".

In the United Kingdom, it was a little easier, and by the time we relocated to Australia, I reacted to almost any version of my name. They call me "Enrika", "Henny", "Hendo" and even "Grethel" (because I look and sound German). My daughter had the same experiences, and our surname was even affectionately pronounced as "Juice-T" by her friends.

Rest assured that you are not alone. This issue is shared by all migrants, whether you are Chinese, Italian, German, Greek, or African.

Some Asian migrants even go as far as to adopt a western name to make it easier in the workplace. It is not uncommon for them to have two different names. The movie star Jackie Chan is a well-known name in the Western world, but in China, he is addressed as "Cheng Long". The Taiwanese presidential candidate Eric Chu is called "Chu-Li-Luan" in Chinese.

Western names are widely used by migrants, in addition to their original names. These alternative names are not used for official documents and identification, though. If your name and surname are not well-known and easy to pronounce, be prepared to spell them to everybody. Face-to-face communication is easier because you can provide the person with some sort of identification, e.g. your driver's licence. However, telephonic communication is more challenging. If your email address starts with your name and surname and you need to spell it over the phone, make sure to pack a truckload of patience and tact in your lunchbox every day.

Top tip: *Learn the NATO phonetic alphabet to make the process a bit easier and less frustrating for both yourself and the recipient on the other end of the line. Either that or you should consider changing or shortening your name to save yourself a lifetime of frustration.*

Numbers are another sticky point. Some migrants may struggle with words with the th-sound: "that", "Thor" and "thread". When you provide your postcode over the phone, and you say "three" the other person hears "free". After fifteen years of living in English-speaking countries, I still can't distinguish or hear the difference between "fifteen" or "fifty". I avoid embarrassment and awkwardness at supermarkets and shop checkouts by making sure that I can visually see the total amount on the register.

Making **appointments** via the telephone can also create some embarrassing "migration moments". Always check if you have heard the time for an appointment correctly.

Australians still use "am" and "pm" for indicating time because they use the 12-hour clock system, which runs from 1am to 12 noon and then from 1pm to 12 midnight. If you come from a country where the 24-hour clock is commonly used, this is a recipe for many misunderstandings. Also, note how they write the time. There is no space between the number and the abbreviation (1pm instead of 1 pm).

I had the experience where a friend said that I should be at her house for "Tea" at eight. I couldn't figure out why we were having tea at 8am? After several days I called her again to find out if I had lost my marbles. It seemed that I was invited for dinner at 8pm. If Australians ask: "What you are making for tea?" or "What's for tea?", they want to know what you're cooking for dinner.

Some Australians have a British background, and they might say "half 8", which means 8:30 and not 7:30 (as in some languages). When making appointments, always repeat the time to the person to ensure there are no misunderstandings. You will usually wait for medical practitioners but being there an

hour too early is not funny. Embrace new technology and book all your medical appointments online with the HealthEngine app:
www.healthengine.com.au/app-download

Real-life story

A Dutch friend and her family, with the surname "Breed" (means "wide" in Dutch) lived in the United States for several years. They were endlessly teased because Americans thought it meant "to breed". Their move to France couldn't come soon enough!

PRONUNCIATION

If you speak your mother-tongue at home, it is highly unlikely that you will ever lose your accent. Unknown to me, my accent and pronunciation of certain words were the office joke for several months.

I couldn't then and still can't pronounce the "sph"-sound. Our local coffee shop close to the office was "The Sphinx". Every time when new employees started working at our office, they came to me to ask where they could buy coffee. It was only when one of my new colleagues couldn't keep a straight face and burst out laughing, that I realised what was going on. I laughed too, but I felt embarrassed and ashamed and a whole lot of resentment towards the instigator.

That evening at home, I cried my eyes out. I couldn't believe that somebody could be so mean and cruel. I realised very quickly that every migrant would have their own unique "migrant experiences" and that you can learn from it, or you could keep on being the depressed migrant victim.

You are not alone in this predicament. Many fellow migrants go through the same pronunciation "agony", which, for them, is mostly far worse than for some of us.

On the day of our arrival in the United Kingdom, my husband and daughter went to the local supermarket to buy groceries. When they left the supermarket, my daughter asked my husband what language the cashier was speaking. The Surrey-accent was new to her, and she had to get used to all the new accents in the United Kingdom.

Most migrants, however, will tell you that they have no issues listening to and understanding other people. As mentioned in previous chapters, migrants are more consciously aware of differences and therefore, more attuned to different accents.

In a country which is built on migration, most Australians have a condition called **"accent deafness"**. Lynne Murphy, professor of linguistics at the University of Sussex, concluded that accent deafness is more attributed to inattention. People can hear the differences between the accents; it just takes a lot of conscious effort. It is not because Australians are rude or doing it on purpose to annoy you. Research shows that accent deafness is also common with Americans. Migrants are just more aware of the accent differences due to their daily awareness of being misunderstood.

Another theory is that due to the melting pot of different cultures and languages in Australia, one tends to become deaf to dialectical differences. Some people can identify your accent immediately, while others may identify it as Swedish, Dutch, German or even coming from New-Zealand. A British colleague described my accent very eloquently as "colonial". Either way, to our frustration, we still sometimes end up with the wrong pizza order or a completely different cup of coffee.

The flip side of the coin is that you will also meet people who love your accent. We have colleagues who don't want us to stop talking and our children's friends love the accent.

Real-life story

A friend who recently visited a dietician shared a story, which is an excellent example of how communication gaps and miscommunications are created due to language differences.

She explained to the dietician that she only eats two slabs of chocolates a day (in her home country, it meant two blocks/pieces of chocolate).

The dietician was horrified and shocked (because, for an Australian, a slab of chocolate is a whole bar of chocolate and not only just two pieces).

LINGUISTIC LONGING

Your mother-tongue or native language is the language that you have been exposed to since your conception, after your birth and within the first critical period of years when your language skills have developed. It is usually the language that a person learned as a child at home from their parents or primary care-givers. Children growing up in bilingual homes can, according to this definition, have more than one mother tongue or native language.

Your mother-tongue is thus an integral part of a child's personal, social and cultural identity. It also brings about the reflection and learning of successful social patterns of acting and speaking.

If you are an extrovert and use your whole body and face to communicate, your biggest challenge could be to learn English expressions to relay the emotions you are trying to communicate. Sometimes, when you do find an English expression with more or less the same meaning, it doesn't have the same emotional connection, or it lacks the feeling you want to express. Barkhuizen and Knoch describe this phenomenon as "linguistic longing".

Some migrants describe this feeling as if they have a split personality. A Czech proverb states: "Learn a new language and get a new soul." Research has shown that people speaking more than one language can literally change their personalities or the way they communicate as they switch over to another language.

As a South African Australian who speaks English to colleagues and friends, I am, for example, more of an introvert, more reserved and dislike calling people on the phone. As a South African Australian who speaks Afrikaans to friends and family, I am more of an extrovert and bubbly, outgoing and more relaxed. It is normal. You don't have a mental illness!

The comedian, Trevor Noah, brilliantly explains this phenomenon in this Facebook clip:

www.facebook.com/watch/?v=2148414191931399

Top tip: *Make a list of the expressions you use most in your mother-tongue and learn the English or Australian equivalent. Unfortunately, in some cases, there isn't an equivalent.*

IMMIGRANT, AM I

As a non-English speaker, you will have a tougher time with integration. Not only do you need to expand your English and Australian slang vocabulary on a daily basis, but your brain is also continuously in translating mode. This, in itself, is exhausting and energy-draining.

You may know the professional sector or subject-related English (jargon) for your occupation, but most non-English speaking migrants struggle with "social" English.

In your home country, everyday activities, like visiting a medical practitioner or practising your religion, day-to-day banter and joking with friends, came automatically. You didn't have to think about it because you were operating on auto-pilot mode (unconscious competence).

In Australia, everyday activities might become a big issue. You will struggle to do basic things such as tell personal stories or talk about events that happened to you. Don't you believe me? Try describing a recent car accident to your spouse or partner as if you are on the phone, talking to the insurance company. See how well you are doing before you pull out the dictionary or the mobile phone.

As if the daily language struggle is not enough, your children will start correcting your grammar, pronunciation and the idiomatic expressions you use.

There is absolutely no point in resisting their attempts to help you become a better Aussie. Children are quicker to integrate, and they learn language nuances much easier than their adult parents. By correcting you, they are just trying to help because they don't want you to make a fool of yourself.

As a parent, this can be a humbling experience. You need to prepare yourself for how you are going to react to your children's language "lessons". Make it positive moments to learn and also to boost your children's self-esteem and efforts.

After all, you are working as a team, and you need to have each other's backs.

For those parents who want to enrol their children in additional lessons to continue learning their mother tongue, we ask you to consider the following:

It's mostly the parents that want to keep their children's proficiency at a specific level. The children aren't motivated and see it as a punishment. Relax and enjoy speaking your mother-tongue at home and with family and friends in your home country. In the end, healthy relationships with your children are more important than correct spelling and grammar.

It would be accurate to say when you start dreaming in English, that your brain has made the switch. We recently talked to a migrant maths teacher who said it took her seven years to make the transition. She could finally teach without translating concepts and terminology from her native language to English.

English speakers, and family and friends back home, can't comprehend how much this process alone takes from your daily energy levels. At the end of the day, you are exhausted!

When you are in a "fight, flight or freeze" situation, the brain automatically reverts to the mother-tongue. This is not very helpful in the workplace where you are supposed to be a professional! The only way to succeed in these situations is to manage your anxiety and stress levels.

Real-life story

A colleague once shared a painful, defining moment from her school years. She was born and raised in Poland until they fled to Italy. She spent most of her primary school years in Italy while speaking Polish at home. During her secondary school years, her parents decided to immigrate and settle in Australia. One day she had to present a speech in the English class. She started off in English, but as soon as the anxiety kicked in, she started using Italian, Polish and English words. The teacher immediately pulled her from the class, and she had to continue her secondary school years with the international students who were still learning English.

RELIGION

Religious vocabulary and terminology are the most difficult things to change. Many migrants will pray and worship in their mother-tongue until they die. Religious institutions have services in various languages, and it is common to have services in other languages like Mandarin, Cantonese, Spanish, Italian and Greek. It depends mainly on the demographic profile of the community.

If you are religious and want to be part of such a community, be open and honest and tell people, for example, that you struggle to pray in English. Most people will accommodate you and even encourage you to try.

Real-life story

Hindsight is golden, they say. A Greek Australian admitted that he insisted that his family continue to attend the Greek Orthodox Church after their arrival in Australia.

As their children integrated and assimilated into Australian society, they couldn't understand the Greek sermons anymore. This, in turn, created resentment in the children, and as adults, none of his children is practising Christians anymore.

He acknowledged that his stubbornness to attend an English church hurt his children's spiritual journey and thus had a ripple effect on his grandchildren as well.

WHEN ENGLISH IS NOT ENGLISH ANYMORE

Upon our arrival in Australia, we struggled to get our heads around the Aussie slang. Why can't they just call a biscuit a biscuit? What on earth is a "bickie"? An umbrella is a "brolly" and flip-flops are called "thongs". Come on Australia, really!?

Melbourne is pronounced as "Mel-bin" and remember to flatten your "a"-vowels – "I paaarked my caaaar in the caaarpaark."

The French word "crèche" is pronounced as some sort of a mix between "crochet" and "crash". It sounds something like "crachet". "Debut" is pronounced as "deboe" which will make any full-blooded Frenchman cringe.

We've seen British colleagues trying to re-educate the Australians without any success. They only managed to make themselves unpopular and the target of Aussie banter. You just have to go with the flow, even though it goes against every fibre of your being and what your English teachers tried so hard to teach you at school. When in Australia, do as the Aussies do!

THE BENEFITS OF BILINGUALISM

Being bilingual or even multi-lingual has its challenges, but there are many benefits to being bilingual and raising bilingual children. As adults, learning a second language improves your memory and multitasking abilities as well as your attention span and focus.

You'll also be used to switching between different languages depending on the context. This linguistic flexibility helps your brain to adapt easily to change, meaning that new or unfamiliar situations – even ones that have nothing to do with language – don't feel as challenging as they otherwise might.

Benefits for your children

1. Bilingual children can often concentrate better, have better analytical skills and are better at multitasking, due to the strengthening of the dorsolateral prefrontal cortex section of the brain.
2. They have a better sense of self-worth, identity and belonging. This includes feeling good about their cultural heritage and minority language, feeling confident about communicating and connecting with extended family members, and being able to enjoy art, music, movies, and literature in more than one language.
3. They have the possibility of diverse career opportunities later in life.

Benefits for your family

1. Bilingualism improves communication among your family members.

2. It makes it easier for you and your children to be part of your culture and boosts your family's sense of cultural identity and belonging.
3. It creates healthy, complex, and actively engaged brain functioning.

Benefits for the wider community
1. Everyone in the community gets a better appreciation of different languages and cultures.
2. Children can more easily travel and work in different countries and cultures in the future.
3. Children understand and appreciate different cultures.

BILINGUALS ARE SMARTER AND HEALTHIER (SO THEY SAY!)

For non-English speakers, there is more good news. Speaking two languages rather than just one has obvious practical benefits in an increasingly globalised world. However, scientists have proven that the advantages of bilingualism are even more fundamental than being able to communicate with a wider range of people.

Being bilingual makes you smarter. It can have a profound effect on your brain, improving cognitive skills not related to language and even shielding against dementia in old age.

The key difference between bilinguals and monolinguals is as basic as a heightened ability to monitor the environment. Albert Costa, a researcher at the University of Pompeu Fabra in Spain, stated that bilinguals have to switch languages quite often and it, therefore, requires a speaker to keep track of changes of their surroundings in the same way that they monitor their surroundings when driving.

In a study comparing German-Italian bilinguals with Italian monolinguals on monitoring tasks, Mr Costa and his colleagues found that the bilingual subjects not only performed better, but they also did so with less activity in parts of the brain involved in monitoring, indicating that they were more efficient at it.

The effects also extend into the twilight years. In a recent study of 44 elderly Spanish-English bilinguals, scientists, led by the neuropsychologist Tamar Gollan of the University of California, San Diego, found that individuals with a higher degree of bilingualism were more resistant than others to the onset of dementia and other symptoms of Alzheimer's disease. The higher the degree of bilingualism, the later the age of onset.

BILINGUALISM COMES WITH A WARNING SIGN

One of the biggest "pet peeves" of Australians are when people talk to each other in their own language, and others don't know what they are saying. They don't know if they are privately criticising those around them or poking fun at them.

As migrants, we know exactly how it feels and yet we do the same to the Australians. We can't count the number of times we had to ask fellow countrymen to speak English when Australians join a conversation.

Hearing people speak a language you don't understand can be intimidating. Natalie Satakovski used the following example: *"If you feel self-conscious about your outfit on any given day and you step onto a tram full of tourists, some of whom are laughing, you may start to wonder if they're laughing at you."*

People forget that this is exactly how non-English speakers feel all the time. It is, unfortunately, not an excuse to be rude, exclusive, and intolerant.

Be a proud bilingual. Don't let a "migration moment" or "faux pas" deter you from learning and moving forward. Be accommodating and considerate, and you will speak Australian English very deliciously... oops, we mean fluently, in no time!

SUMMARY OF RECOMMENDATIONS

1. Make life easier for yourself and adopt either a shorter version of your name or use your middle name if it is easier to pronounce. Don't torture the barista who takes your coffee order with your real name. "Anna" or "Peter" will suffice.

2. Speaking your mother-tongue at home is essential; we are not suggesting at all that you become an English-speaking family when you migrate. It is important to keep in touch with family and friends in your mother-tongue. Language is not only a way to communicate, but it also creates and strengthens an emotional bond with people.

3. Read Australian newspapers. Subscribe to a "Word of the day" app or website. If you don't know a word, look it up. Prepare yourself with written notes when you visit the doctor. Always use a grammar check when typing emails and other professional documents.

4. Watch television programs like *The Project* and *Have you been paying attention*? Aussie banter is part of the make-up of these programs. Watch Australian movies like *Red Dog, The Castle* and *Crocodile Dundee*, to learn about Aussie culture and slang.

5. Buy a pocket Aussie slang dictionary and study it every day.

6. Be considerate to fellow Australians who don't speak or understand your mother-tongue.

7. Be kind to yourself and your family. Rome wasn't built in a day, and the same goes for building a new life (and vocabulary) in Australia. It takes time, patience and lots of energy. Don't sweat the small stuff!

12

TAKING CARE OF YOURSELF AND YOUR FAMILY

"Rest and self-care are so important. When you take time to replenish your spirit, it allows you to serve others from the overflow. You cannot serve from an empty vessel."

~ Eleanor Brown
(American novelist, anthologist, editor and speaker)

For most migrants, especially migrant women, self-care is a foreign concept. No, it is not New Age mumbo-jumbo! It is a very important part of taking care of ourselves, but it was rarely taught or modelled during childhood.

For the most part, our own mothers and grandmothers provided us with examples of selfless women who sacrificed their own needs, interests, health and financial independence for their husbands, children and wider community. They never took time for relaxation, nor did they actively practice replenishing themselves.

Years ago, a food commercial nailed this lack of self-care in a brilliant way:

The scene: A family sits around the dining room table. The children ask their grandmothers questions on how they filled their days in the "old days".

Child 1: "What did you do all day when you were younger?"

Granny 1: "We cooked and cooked and cooked."

Child 2 (very surprised): "Really? But what did you do for fun?"

Granny 2 (with a big smile): "Ah ... we baked."

WHAT IS SELF-CARE?

Among all the different women we have met, we have found that most women internalise their guilt about self-care. Guilt for taking time and guilt using money exclusively for themselves. These women see self-care as employing a part-time housekeeper or going for a facial every six weeks.

Patti Clark, an expert in self-care for women, says that women find it challenging to take time for themselves and prioritise self-care. It often takes an illness or an accident, or the stress related to migration to persuade them to give themselves the time and care they need.

When you ask migrant women what they do to relax, most of them can't tell you. Some have hobbies like quilting or organising a walking group. But most go from home to work, to shops to home – day after day after day. They cook, clean, wash and iron, drive children around, feed the pets and help out at the local charity or church.

However, it is acceptable for their husbands to join friends and colleagues for a drink after work or play golf on weekends. The children are allowed to have a social life and some much-needed downtime during weekends and school holidays.

Mom is always last on every list.

SOCIAL READJUSTMENT RATING SCALE

You may be the most organised and "with it" person for kilometres around, but that doesn't mean you don't need self-care. With migration, there are so many different stressors as mentioned in previous chapters.

Stress can be experienced on different levels, and as a migrant, you may encounter several stressors, like:
1. unforeseen or unpredictable crises,
2. major life events like marriage, death, or birth,
3. daily hassles, also known as micro stressors (daily annoyances),
4. ambient stressors like noise, traffic, and overcrowding, and
5. organisational stressors, for example, conflict at work or a toxic workplace.

How do we measure stress levels, and how do we know if they are eustress (positive) or distress (negative)? Life events scales can be useful to assess stressful things that people experience in their lives. One such scale is the Social Readjustment Rating Scale (SRRS).

The SRRS scale was developed by psychiatrists Thomas Holmes and Richard Rahe, to weigh the impact of life events. They listed 43 events.

Event	Value	Event	Value
Death of a spouse	100	Change in responsibilities at work	29
Divorce	73	Child leaving home	29
Marital separation	65	Trouble with in-laws	29
Imprisonment	63	Outstanding personal achievement	28
Death of a close family member	63	Spouse starts or stops work	26
Personal injury or illness	53	Begin or end school	26
Marriage	50	Change in living conditions	25
Dismissal from work	47	Revision of personal habits	24
Marital reconciliation	45	Trouble with boss	23
Retirement	45	Change in working hours/conditions	20
Change in health of family member	44	Change in residence	20
Pregnancy	40	Change in schools	20
Sexual difficulties	39	Change in recreation	19
Gain a new family member	39	Change in church activities	19
Business readjustment	39	Change in social activities	18
Change in financial state	38	Minor mortgage or loan	17
Death of a close friend	37	Change in sleeping habits	16
Change to different line of work	36	Change in number of family reunions	15
Change in frequency of arguments	35	Change in eating habits	14
Major mortgage	32	Vacation	13
Foreclosure of mortgage or loan	30	Minor violation of law	10

To calculate your score, you add up the number of "life change units" if an event occurred in the past year. A score of more than 300 means that individual is at risk for illness, a score between 150 and 299 means risk of illness is moderate, and a score under 150 means that individual only has a slight risk of illness.

You will notice that migration is not even listed on this scale. However, if you calculate some of the events listed that are related to migration, you could easily end up with a score of 300 plus.

With migration, there is also information overload when you first arrive in the country, new road signs, food labels, billboards – everything needs reading and understanding. You might even be doing this in a language other than English!

Dr Barbara Markway explains that when we are stressed out, self-care is often the first thing we let go.

We do that because our brains go into "fight, flight or freeze" mode and our perspective immediately narrow. This narrow perspective makes us think that we don't have many options.

We are so busy trying to solve problems that we're stuck in "doing mode" (trying to get more and more done). By switching to "being mode," you may just get the break you need. If we know we have options to cope with stress, we immediately feel better.

DISTINCT STRESSORS FOR MIGRANTS

As mentioned in Chapter 8, migration and the additional cultural shock may have three different outcomes during the adjustment phase.

Culture shock is not necessarily only negative. It may also be a positive, creative force with an educational impact to motivate personal growth and enhance the individual's self-awareness. You have the opportunity to reinvent yourself, start a new career or hobby or be the person you always wanted to be. However, culture shock may also aggravate the stress levels in a family. As the authors of this book, we feel we have a responsibility to enlighten you to the following stressors that are very prevalent and specific to migrants in Australia.

Challenged morals and values

About a year after our arrival in Australia, a friend described her biggest issue with migration as follows: *"You don't know if you are coming or going, what to stand for and what to fall for when you arrive in Australia. It's almost like building a new identity and personality from scratch again."*

Another explained it as feeling *"like a deer in the headlights; things are coming at you at such a speed, you don't know where to turn."*

My friends were spot on with their remarks. Suddenly, things that were taboo and even unthinkable in your home country, are perfectly acceptable here in Australia, for example:

- Your best friend may have tattoos all over his or her body, and the most amazing thing is that he or she is such a lovely and decent person.

- Most of your colleagues are living with their partners in *de facto*-relationships and never intend to get married.

- Every third expression of disgust or irritation is: "Oh my God!", "Jesus!" or "Christ!" and people are openly atheist or non-religious.

- At school, they teach your children to relax through mindfulness and meditation.

- At the office party, your religious views about alcohol and food such as beef and pork are dismissed or not even considered.

Be prepared that your morals, values, customs, and religion will be questioned and will be challenged, more frequently than ever before.

Egalitarian (classless) society

Australia is a very egalitarian (classless) society. This is a result of the very humble beginnings as a convict colony. It is completely different from other societies.

The house you lived in, the cars you drove, your social status or your extensive network of influential people you knew in your home country may have provided you with a certain amount of security, identity and status.

In Australia, you are not going to impress the Aussies with these things. In fact, you will just get the opposite feedback. Australians don't care who you rubbed shoulders with in the past, how much money you have, your postcode or even your professional status. You will have friends from all walks of life, and it is not unusual to see best mates, a truck-driver, and a lawyer, having a beer together at a social event.

There is no such thing as "cheap labour" in Australia. A plumber might be earning just as much as a lawyer and even have a few investment properties. Australians are prepared to give anybody a fair go. Until you have citizenship, see yourself as a very welcome guest in Australia. Aussies want to know the real, authentic, and vulnerable you.

Housing

In Australia, people also built with bricks, but after the Second World War and the massive influx of European migrants, Australia had a housing crisis. They started building with wooden frames to keep up with the increasing demand. Brick houses are fairly old and old-fashioned and are usually not up to some migrants' standards.

Many migrants will start off by renting a house. Building and owning your own home can take from a year to two years. The Australian government is also making it more and more difficult for non-residents or non-citizens to buy houses.

In recent years, many overseas nationals started to pay top dollars for the fresh air in Australia. This increased house prices in such a way that buying a house are beyond the reach of the average Australian. You need to at least have permanent residency before you can buy a house, or you can buy a home "off-plan" – prior to building commencing by around two years.

The good news is that in many instances you may be

eligible for the "First-time home-owners' grant", which can be around $20 000. Financial institutions are hesitant to provide home loans to older people. In fact, it is considered unethical by the banks to grant you a home loan beyond your retirement age. If you are 45 years old, chances are you will find it difficult to get a 30-year loan.

Some migrants have high expectations, and they want to have the same housing they had in their home country. This, however, puts a lot of unnecessary pressure on families. Many Australians rent a home for their entire lives – it is a common phenomenon (same as in Europe). It is every Aussie's dream to own his or her own "castle", but you also need to be practical. Depending on your age when migrating to Australia, owning a property is not necessarily a given.

Cleaning

Migrants or ex-pats who lived in countries where housekeepers, gardeners, drivers, and au pairs were an everyday luxury, do underestimate the amount of energy it takes to clean a house, to cook and maintain a big garden. If your children are used to a housekeeper doing everything for them, you should be prepared to either become their cleaner or brace yourselves for some major power struggles when arriving in Australia. The older your children are when you emigrate from your home country, the harder it will be to change deep-rooted habits.

Unfortunately, many wives are bearing the brunt of cleaning. If the spouse or partner is working full-time and the children are at school, the wife ends up being the housekeeper, cleaner and gardener.

Australian cleaners charge on average about $50 per hour. If they clean your home for four hours, it totals at $200.

Migration is a particularly good opportunity to get the whole family into the habit of doing daily chores. Another reason for doing chores at home is because it sets your family up for success at the office and at school.

It is unlikely that in the office you will have some fairies come in and clean your desk, make coffee or tea, or clean the kitchen. Most workplaces have rotating cleaning rosters where all colleagues get a chance to do their bit to clean the office and kitchen. After a meeting during lunch, everybody will automatically start cleaning up, washing the dishes, and putting electronic equipment away, if needed.

Schools organise Working Bee-days, where parents and kids must pitch in with maintenance and cleaning of the school grounds and buildings.

School and community events

At an event, you will most probably receive a "snag". A snag is a pork sausage, folded in a slice of white bread and served on a serviette. The bread is usually not buttered, and you may choose if you want fried onions and tomato sauce (ketchup) with your snag.

Australians are modest, unpretentious people. They are not unsophisticated; they are just more practical than some other cultures. They save labour by not washing up hundreds of plates and save the environment from hundreds of plastic plates being thrown into rubbish bins.

Tea and coffee are served in mugs (most of the time it is an odd assortment of mugs) with the teabag still inside and a piece of cake on a serviette. At coffee shops, you can bring your "keep cup" for your daily coffee shot to reduce the environmental impact of take-way cups. If you feel that the Australians are not up to your high standards, don't make enemies by voicing your judgement out loud!

Health problems or other special needs

Expect the medical system to be different from what you are used to from your home country. If you or a family member has a health problem, a physical disability, or if your child has special learning needs, adjusting to life in Australia may be especially challenging.

Before you have PR or citizenship, you may need to pay for expensive treatment or services yourself. Make sure that these costs are accounted for in the monthly budget.

However, after obtaining PR or citizenship, you can change your mindset of always having to pay for yourself or get things done on your own. You are paying taxes, and the Australian government has various schemes in place to lift the financial burden or to provide services to assist you or your family on the journey.

This might not necessarily only be a financial burden but could also be in the form of a nurse or carers to visit you at home to help with medical needs or give you a shower.

A friend who recently welcomed her second baby reminded us again on how important it is to reiterate this with our readers. On enquiring how they are doing, she replied with the following text message (shortened): *"We are doing okay. Nurses say I am not asking for enough help. Ten years in Australia, and I still have to remind myself to open my mouth and just ask for assistance."*

Rigid stereotypes

As a migrant who recently arrived in Australia, you may still have very fixed mindsets on gender roles, social class, mental health, religion, and sexual orientation, which originated from your country of origin.

In Australia, labelling is very fluid and ever-changing. It is not uncommon to have a male nurse attending to your personal needs while in a hospital or seeing a stay-at-home dad taking his children to school or swimming lessons. Stay-at-home dads are becoming such a common phenomenon in Australia, that Channel 9 produced a drama series called *House Husbands*.

In 2016, the Australian Bureau of Statistics released information on how work has changed in Australia:

- 24% of mothers stay at home,
- 6% of fathers stay at home,
- 10% of all fathers work part-time to spend more time with their families, and
- 14% of all fathers work less than 35 hours per week.

Australian women have rights and are not seen as extensions

of somebody's ego or as second-class citizens. They are individuals who add value to the workplace and their community. Some companies or organisations may still have a culture of the "old boys club", but this is rapidly changing. There are so many opportunities for women. If you apply yourself, you will find an audience of women supporting (and celebrating) your journey.

On arrival in Australia, it is even likely that the wife may be the main breadwinner. Her skills, knowledge and profession could be more in demand than the husband's more specific career. Many migrant wives are employed while their husbands may struggle to find employment.

For most migrant men, this situation is too much to handle, and many marriages have bitten the dust. Fixed mindsets about manhood and gender roles are not helping marriages, relationships, and families to grow and flourish in Australia. For most men, it is a very humbling experience, and it is strongly recommended to address any such issues with a trained professional, as soon as possible.

Men, in general, are in denial when it comes to mental health issues such as depression, feelings of low self-worth and suicidal thoughts. Don't wait until it is too late! You and your family decided to immigrate to Australia for a better life – not a broken family.

Under-employment

A quick reminder again about the "stepping back in time" phenomenon. If you were a CEO in your home country, it is not a given that you are going to walk into an Australian workplace on the same level. This only happens if you are head-hunted and recruited for a specific position or skillset. Many migrants are under-employed or over-qualified for their first job.

Under-employment refers to any of the following scenarios:

1. **"Over-qualification"** or **"over-education"** or the employment of workers with high education skills levels,

or experience in jobs that do not require such abilities.
For example, a trained medical doctor with a foreign credential who works as a taxi driver.

2. **"Involuntary part-time"** work, where workers who could (and would like to) be working for a full workweek can only find part-time work.

3. **"Overstaffing"** or **"hidden unemployment"** or "disguised unemployment" (also called "labour hoarding"), the practice in which businesses employ workers who are not fully occupied—for example, seasonal fruit pickers in Australia.

Remember, it is not the end of the world if you are under-employed or over-qualified at first. See it as a stepping stone and learning curve towards your next great job. Work with a plan and make any training or re-education part of the family's goal setting and future planning.

Work-life balance

Many migrants are soldier-on, hard-working people who want to get the job done and build their new future. Even when they are as sick as a dog, they will drag themselves out of bed and go to work. Migrants appreciate the opportunities they have been given, and they don't take anything for granted.

Australians, however, are genuinely concerned about their work-life balance. In broad terms, it basically means that if your job requires you to work eight hours a day, you work eight hours a day. They work hard during the day, but they believe they also have a personal life and a family that needs their attention.

Depending on the company or organisation you work for, it is a general unwritten rule. People don't work overtime, they don't take work home, and they definitely don't work on weekends. It will be frowned upon, and some Aussies may even become suspicious if you continue with your old ways.

Don't be surprised when a fellow colleague tells you that

they are selling or storing all their belongings to embark on a world tour because they want to live their dream while they still have their good health to enjoy it.

Fellow migrants take a very deep breath and "take a chill pill" as the Aussies would say. Relax and give yourself time to settle in. You don't need to build Rome in one week, and you don't need to impress anybody. Your physical and mental health is more important, and family always comes first. Do what makes you happy. That is the Aussie way!

We still meet migrants who have lived in Australia for several years and are still trapped in the mindset of going home after work to their safe space, shut the doors and keep the outside world out. Don't get stuck in survival mode. As soon as you are settled give yourself the time and space to enjoy the fabulous parks, recreational activities, and the fabulous Australian lifestyle!

SUPPORT ON YOUR MIGRATION JOURNEY

Think about your support network in your home country. Maybe your parents were living next door or close by. You had a big, supportive group of friends who took turns to drive the children to activities after school. You socialised with your girlfriends while the kids were playing or doing after-school activities.

In the evenings, you got home, and the house was clean, the washing had been done, and the housekeeper had started with dinner before she left. Once a week, you met with a care group from your religious affiliation where you maybe prayed together and supported each other. Your life, back home, was running like a well-oiled machine.

Now, you are in Australia, and suddenly your support network is gone. You sometimes look at your spouse or partner and think: "How did I manage back home with this level of emotional support?" or you look at the pile of laundry and think: "Why did I do this to myself?"

Due to time differences and distance, your supports are now not a phone call or a quick coffee away anymore. You may feel extremely lonely and isolated, and most of the time you will be too proud to ask for help or admit that you are in desperate need of a hug or just a cup of coffee with a friend willing to listen. This will make you vulnerable.

The management of your stress levels and the creation of a new support network in Australia is going to be key to your family's failure or success. The same scenario applies to spouses or partners and children.

Creating a support network
Not all of us are spontaneous extroverts who thrive on meeting new people or embarking on new adventures all the time.

If you are single or an introvert and you struggle to reach out, the following ideas may be useful:
1. Attend events, like concerts, BBQ's and networking opportunities of fellow countrymen and artists (find them on social media).
2. Join your local religious organisation or group.
3. Join like-minded groups of people who share the same hobbies, a book club, or a language conversation group on Meetup (www.meetup.com).
4. Join local groups or attend events organised by the local council or community organisations.
5. Join support groups, for example, support for parents with autistic children. Find a specific support group by searching on the internet for "support group + [your interest]".
6. Start to volunteer.
7. Take part in community or school events.
8. Join a local sport club or walking group.

Most meetup or support groups have no membership fee, but some may ask a monthly or annual membership fee. These fees are not expensive. The most important thing is that you get out of your comfort zone or self-imposed isolation and meet other people. Initially, it is hard work to make new friends. Remember, in order to have good friends; you also need to be a good friend.

Asking for help and support

You can minimise the culture shock and make the transition easier if you ask for help when you need it. We are not saying that you should go knocking on your neighbour's door all the time! There is support and assistance available everywhere if you just know where to start looking. Asking for help is a sign of self-awareness, resilience, and maturity. It is not a sign of weakness.

During the first year or two after your arrival in Australia, you will need to monitor not only your own but also your family's mental health and stress levels.

Symptoms of culture shock and integration stress may include:
- Anger
- Boredom
- Compulsive eating/drinking/weight gain
- Desire/severe longing for home and old friends
- Excessive concern over cleanliness or excessive sleep
- Feelings of helplessness
- Getting "stuck" on one thing
- Glazed stare
- Homesickness
- Hostility towards host nationals
- Impulsivity
- Irritability
- Mood swings
- Physiological stress reactions
- Stereotyping host nationals
- Suicidal or fatalistic thoughts
- Withdrawal

In all our years of assisting migrants, we've only once heard of suicide as a direct result of migration.

However, many migrants have mental health issues like depression and anxiety. Marriages end up in divorce for reasons like spouses or partners refusing to change their traditional views or be more accommodating and less rigid, unmet emotional needs, abuse (emotional or financial) and infidelity.

Don't start looking for help when the wheels are already falling off. Educate yourself about the warning signs and ask for assistance well in advance.

Life Coaching:
If you need assistance with your career, relationships, goals, happiness, or even finding your life's purpose, integration or even re-inventing yourself, you could engage a life coach. A life coach is someone who assists people with identifying and reaching goals. They motivate and encourage their clients to achieve positive change in either their professional or personal lives. Coaching is future-focused, and the emphases are on action, accountability and tangible outcomes.

Contact www.pillarsofpillars.com.au to find out how they can assist you. If they can't help you, they will be able to refer you to a life coach who specialises in your specific need.

Counselling:
Counselling, on the other hand, is a therapy that deals with healing pain, dysfunction and conflict within an individual or in relationships. It often focuses on resolving difficulties arising from the past that hampers an individual's emotional functioning in the present, improving overall psychological functioning and dealing with the present in more emotionally healthy ways.

The best thing about Australia is that every organisation is online, and information is easily accessible. If you don't have an internet connection at home, you can access the internet at your local library. You can find help on the internet via social media, at local councils, community centres and via a telephone line.

In the past, seeking professional help was expensive, tedious, and time-consuming. One of the great advantages of online counselling is how convenient and flexible it can be. You can start a session anywhere, at any time, if you have a device that can connect to the internet.

The two organisations listed below have been used with great success by migrants. For many people, it takes away barriers they may have in accessing services such as mobility, travelling and waiting lists.

Betterhelp is an American-based, online counselling service you can access anytime and anywhere. They will match you with an independently certified counsellor that is there to help you no matter your needs. They'll stay with you unless you decide to change. Get feedback, advice, and guidance from your counsellor via video chats, text messages and email.

Couple counselling is also available to migrants who have moved abroad together. You receive unlimited sessions around the clock at an affordable, flat monthly fee. Message your counsellor wherever you are, on-site or through the app: www.betterhelp.com

Counselling Online is a program funded by the Australian Government Department of Health and is operated by Turning Point. This service is free, other than any data costs you may incur from your internet service provider: www.counsellingonline.org.au

Mental Health Organisations:
Beyondblue, an Australian not-for-profit organisation, provides information, surveys, subject-specific articles, a helpline and heaps of helpful tools and resources to assist anybody. Their website: www.beyondblue.org.au

Other organisations that are worth mentioning are:
- Lifeline: 13 11 14
- Kids helpline: 1800 551 800
- Mensline Australia: 1800 187 263
- PANDA (Perinatal Anxiety and Depression): 1300 726 306

The best thing about Australia is that every organisation is online, and information is easily accessible. If you don't have an internet connection at home, you can access the internet at your local library. You can find help on the internet via social media, at local councils, community centres and via a telephone line.

TOP TIPS FOR SELF-CARE (MEN AND WOMEN)

As mentioned before in this chapter self-care is a vital part of your successful migration and integration journey. It is not only one thing, such as yoga. There are several pathways to self-care.

If possible, a retreat is a lovely way to create time and space for yourself. Hotels often have special promotions, and you can make a booking for some peace and quiet. If those are not options, here are a few other cheaper options:

Sensory self-care:
1. Focus on the sensations around you - sights, smells, sounds - this helps you to be present in the moment.
2. Go for a walk and breathe in the fresh air.
3. Listen to running water.
4. Burn a scented candle.
5. Get a massage or take a hot shower or a relaxing hot bath.
6. Cuddle with a pet or volunteer at an animal shelter.
7. Walk barefoot on the lawn.
8. Appreciate the afternoon sunset.
9. Go for a walk in nature and listen to the calls of the birds.
10. Listen to your favourite music or create a personal playlist.
11. Do some stargazing.

Pleasure self-care:

1. Be creative! Do some art, journal, or play a musical instrument.
2. Do some gardening. Plant flowers even if you are living in a rental property.
3. Take yourself out for a nice meal.
4. Watch a movie.
5. Walk the dogs.
6. Be a tourist in your own city.
7. Pack a picnic basket and relax in your local park.
8. Connect with others – this is an important part of self-care.

Mental self-care:

According to Dr Barbara Markway, the following self-care activities can also boost self-confidence.

1. Clean out a drawer or closet.
2. Simplify your life. Stop multi-tasking.
3. Take one small step on something you've been avoiding.
4. Try something completely new, like Pilates or knitting.
5. Drive to new places and explore.
6. Do a crossword puzzle, Sudoku, or a word search.
7. Read about a new topic.
8. Learn to say no without feeling guilty.
9. Read for pleasure.
10. Don't work late and don't take work home.
11. Work with a life coach/mentor.

Spiritual self-care:

1. Attend church or your place of worship.
2. Read poetry or inspiring quotes.
3. Meditate or pray.
4. Practice gratitude with a gratitude journal.
5. Spend time in nature, go for a walk or hit the beach.
6. Give yourself some spiritual space.

Emotional self-care:
1. Don't label your emotions as "good" or "bad". Feel the emotion, work through it, and try to move on.
2. Accept your feelings.
3. Write your feelings down or draw emoticons in your journal.
4. Cry when you need to.
5. Laugh as much as you can.
6. Practice self-compassion be kind to yourself and give yourself a break.

Physical self-care:
1. Go for a run.
2. Do a workout.
3. Enrol for dancing classes.
4. Go for a bike ride.
5. Get eight hours' sleep every night.
6. Take an afternoon nap, if possible.
7. Men: Treat yourself to a professional close shave.
8. Women: Get a manicure/pedicure.
9. Learn to prepare healthy meals.

Social self-care:
1. Go on a lunch date with a good friend. Face-to-face conversations are especially important.
2. Talk to a friend on the phone.
3. Join a support group.
4. Enjoy quality time with your family.
5. Organise a "men/women only" weekend.
6. Go on a lunch date with your spouse or partner.
7. Take your son/daughter on a special date or experience.

Remember: *Self-care is not self-indulgence. It is self-preservation during the migration stages. Take care of yourself, starting today!*

PRACTICE SELF-CARE WITH CHILDREN

One of Dr Phil McGraw's famous quotes is that children learn what they live, for example, you will not have respectful children if you are not respectful.

As a parent, it is also your job to prepare your children for the next level of life. Teach your children about self-care and model to them how to be a healthy woman or man one day. Instead of preaching it to them, practice it!

You may consider the following suggestions from Carla Birnberg:

1. Create restful moments during your day with the children. Have a proper 15-minute tea break with soothing music or outside in the garden. Take in the fresh air and listen to nature.

2. Play high and low. Everybody must have a high for their day but don't need to have a low.

3. Cook together and try new healthy meals.

4. Clean up together.

5. Ditch screens and start reading. Take turns to choose the book you are reading, almost like a family book club.

6. Create bursts of cardio self-care. Have 60-second dance parties. Create spontaneous movement-breaks during toddler activities or homework sessions. One shouts: "Dance party!" turns on the music and everybody starts dancing.

7. Prioritise serving and helping others. Discuss the good feelings acts of kindness bring to the giver as well. "Service is the rent we pay for living," is a quote of Marian Wright Edelman. Self-care can be as simple as seeing what you can do to help those around you.

8. Play more. Parents, teachers, and coaches can put a lot of pressure on children to perform. Success is important, but

so is playing. Play replenishes creativity and rejuvenates the mind. We know and understand from personal experience that it is difficult to get out of "survival mode" when you are a migrant, but you need to play more.

9. Focus on wings but remind yourself of the roots you've created. Teach your children to have confidence in their choices and to trust their inner voice. By living intuitively (but safely), we develop a feeling of empowerment in our children.

10. Journal with your children. Share hopes and dreams, family goals and answered prayers.

11. Model self-care in your marriage or relationship. Go on date nights. If you can't think of creative date night ideas, visit: www.thedatingdivas.com

12. Replace old rituals with new, creative rituals when you arrive in Australia. For example, birthdays without family sucks but birthday cake for breakfast is awesome!

*The information and advice provided in this chapter are not intended to replace advice from a qualified practitioner. Use these tips as guidelines and to help you find creative ideas.

13

MIGRATORY GRIEF AND LOSS

"Oh, I'm an alien, I'm a legal alien
I'm an Englishman in New York

If "manners maketh man" as someone said
He's the hero of the day
It takes a man to suffer ignorance and smile
Be yourself no matter what they say
Be yourself no matter what they say
Be yourself no matter what they say."

~ Sting
(Lyrics from the song: "Englishman in New York")

Most of our memories, good or bad, are filed in our subconscious, and simple, everyday things can trigger those emotions. The smell of a wood fire could transport you back home immediately, or comfort food may fix most of your homesickness for a while. For every person, the memory trigger is different.

Experiencing grief and loss is part of the immigration journey. It is unfortunately also a subject that we don't like to talk about or share with our loved ones back home. Most news you share with your loved ones back home is sugar-coated to keep up the appearances of your wonderful new life in Australia.

WHAT IS MIGRATORY LOSS?

Michael Cohn, a psychotherapist, says when we think of loss, we think of the loss through the death of people we love. But loss is a far more encompassing theme in our lives. We lose not only through death but also by leaving and being left, by changing and letting go and moving on.

Our losses include not only separation and departures from those we love. There are also conscious and unconscious losses of romantic dreams, impossible expectations, illusions of freedom and power, illusions of safety and the loss of our own younger self. These losses are part of life and are universal, unavoidable, and inexorable. They are necessary because we grow by losing and leaving and letting.

When we migrate, our losses are usually profound, involving many of our life anchors and stabilisers. This typically involves things like the loss of status, family roots, financial certainty, support systems, identity, friendships, language, losses of things known and self-evident, losses of cultural identities and certainties, and self-image and the like.

WHAT IS MIGRATORY GRIEF?

Grief is a natural but multifaceted response to loss. It might be the loss of a loved one, relationship, pregnancy, pet, job, ill-health, or way of life. Other experiences of loss may be due to children leaving home, infertility and separation from friends and family.

We usually focus only on the emotional response to loss, but it also has physical, cognitive, behavioural, social, cultural, spiritual, and philosophical dimensions. The more significant the loss, the more intense the grief is likely to be.

Grief is expressed in many ways, and it can affect every part of your life, your emotions, thoughts and behaviour, beliefs, physical health, your sense of self and identity, and your relationships with others. It can leave you feeling sad, angry, anxious, shocked, regretful, overwhelmed, isolated, irritable, or numb.

Grief has no set pattern. Everyone experiences grief differently. Some people may grieve for weeks and months, while others may describe their grief lasting for years. Through the process of grief, however, you begin to create new experiences and habits that work around your loss.

According to the psychotherapist, Inci T Picard, geographical relocation induces a sense of loss, and the reactions are similar to grief. Picard identified two types of migratory losses:

1. **Physical loss**, which refers to tangible loss, such as loss of a loved one.

2. **Symbolic loss**, which refers to abstract loss, such as loss of a homeland, status, social environment, ego and social identity, which indeed migrants experience the most.

When migrants leave their home country, they are starting to close an important chapter in their lives. Whether they are leaving their home country for economic reasons, war, marriage or education, this process is the same for all migrants.

They desire to establish a new life for themselves and their families. However, confronting the realities may cause deep pain, sadness, loneliness, and grief-like symptoms.

Picard also refers to the work of Parkes, which states that grief is completed in four stages:

- numbness,
- yearning and searching,
- disorganisation and despair, and
- reorganisation.

It is not always easy to reach the last stage of grief where an individual feels interested in life again and is able to move on without what has been lost.

If the grief is unresolved or there is prolonged mourning, there will be an internalisation, which will lead to depression. In other words, the person becomes stuck in the second phase of the grieving process.

THE EFFECTS OF MIGRATORY GRIEF

Grief often resembles depression, and some people do go on to develop depression following a significant loss. If you are dealing with a significant loss and finding it difficult to cope, see your doctor (GP).

Emotions

It is common to cry a lot and feel incredibly sad. Some people never cry at all, but this doesn't mean they are not grieving. There is likely to be initial shock and disbelief as well as a range of feelings, including numbness, a sense of unreality, anger, loneliness, or guilt.

Physical health

Grief can be exhausting, and this may weaken the immune system, making people prone to colds and illness.

Social life

Some people may isolate themselves after losing a loved one. Some solitude may be necessary for healing, but it's also important to stay connected to others.

Spiritual life

Some people may experience dreams about their loved one, feeling their presence or hearing their voice. People who are grieving search for meaning and examine their spiritual beliefs.

Post-traumatic growth

Some people find positive experiences following grief and loss, such as a new sense of wisdom, maturity and meaning in life.

Complicated grief and depression

In some people, grief can be prolonged or more intense, and it may interfere with their ability to cope with everyday life. This might be more likely if the loss was particularly significant.

GETTING THROUGH MIGRATORY GRIEF AND LOSS

Grief is something that takes time to work through. While everyone finds their own way to grieve, it's important to have the support of friends and family or someone else and to talk about your loss when you need to.

1. Don't be afraid to ask for help.
2. Talk to friends and family about how you are feeling or consider joining a support group.
3. Take care of your physical health. Grieving can be exhausting, so it's important to follow a healthy diet, exercise and get enough sleep.
4. Manage your stress. Relaxation and gentle exercise may be helpful.
5. Do things you enjoy, even if you don't really feel like doing them.

Make sure that your general practitioner (GP) knows that you are a newly arrived migrant who is experiencing culture shock and migratory grief and loss. Sometimes you only need to talk to a professional to help you navigate your migratory journey instead of going on medication for depression, anxiety and other related conditions.

To access a mental health care plan, follow the below steps:

1. Book an appointment with your regular GP. When you book, tell them you want to talk about a mental health care plan. That way, the GP will know in advance and be able to set enough time aside.

2. At the appointment, talk to the GP about what's been going on. It helps to be as open as possible. If you're feeling nervous, there's no need to worry – that's a really normal response, but GPS see people for mental health care plans all the time. They're trained to listen, and except for in some special circumstances (which you can ask them about beforehand) what you tell them is confidential.

3. Your GP might ask you to fill out a questionnaire about how you've been feeling to work out the best support for you.

4. Many GPs will ask you to come back for another appointment before they decide whether a mental health care plan is the right thing for you.

Real-life story

Andreas came to Australia from Greece at the age of 14. He didn't know the language but immediately started high school in Perth. It wasn't easy; he was bullied a lot and found it a difficult transition.

They moved from a small Greek island where everyone knew one another to a big city where his family didn't know anyone.

The family experienced tremendous loss and grief, which was never acknowledged or addressed. His father turned to alcohol to numb his grief and manage his depression, which had far-reaching and devasting effects on the whole family.

IS IT DEPRESSION?
Grief and depression are quite different, but they may appear similar as they can both lead to feelings of intense sadness, insomnia, poor appetite, and weight loss.

Depression stands out from grief as being more persistent, with constant feelings of emptiness and despair and a difficulty experiencing pleasure or joy.

If you notice that depression symptoms continue, or your grief begins to get in the way of how you live, work, or share relationships, then it's vital to get support or seek professional help.

Note: *If you decide to seek professional support, make sure to find a practitioner who has been a migrant as well. Second and third-generation Australians can't comprehend the concept of migration, and they will inform you that they can only vaguely remember how their grandparents or parents struggled to adjust. Find somebody who understands you.*

SHARING IN CELEBRATIONS
You are miles away and celebrating a special event with your family is not as easy as jumping into your car and quickly driving there anymore. It is important to keep those family and friendship connections going. To find more ideas, we discuss in this section of the book subscribe to our website and newsletter at www.yourmoveguide.com

The following activities may be helpful to assist you and your family in dealing with "not being there" and "missing out":

Out of sight, out of mind
We have found that the biggest challenge for migrants is to keep those you love in your subconscious mind. It is so easy to drown in all the new information and your new environment. You are exhausted at the end of the day, and it is quite easy to lose sight of reaching out to people in your home country.

Over the years, we have tried several different methods of reaching out. Some were more successful than others. It is all about trial and error to see what works best for you and your family.

Place updated photos of family members and cousins on the fridge. While you are cooking, tell your children stories about each family member and recite their names. When you return to your home country for a visit, they will remember the names and not be shy when they meet again.

If you have a farewell party before your departure, get a cartoonist to draw the faces of everybody who attended. Frame the pictures and hang it in your new home in Australia. You could also have everyone sign a blank poster and have that framed, or even hire a photo booth, which automatically prints two sets of photos.

With social media, it has become so much easier to share in each other's joy and sadness. You can use Facebook or WhatsApp. Create WhatsApp groups, for example:

- Group 1: Mom, sister(s) and yourself
- Group 2: Friends
- Group 3: You and other siblings. If you have brothers, connect with their wives. Women are more inclined to share and keep in contact.
- Group 4: Granny and the grandchildren

Schedule weekly Skype/Zoom/FaceTime or WhatsApp connecting times. We have weekly Sunday evening sessions with the family. Only skip a session when you have another event to attend.

Grandparents can read stories for their grandchildren by pre-recording the reading if you can't do it with Skype or WhatsApp. A good idea is to have the book with the child, and the grandparents have a copy or photos of the text.

Use empty postcards with interesting pictures to write a story for children. Mail it to them. Children love to get mail.

Keep a journal to record your thoughts and feelings, especially if you are unable to sleep.

Birthdays

With my husband's 50th birthday, the family had created a big birthday banner with balloons and put it in the background during the Skype session. He loved it and was very touched by the gesture.

We would recommend, from grandparents or family back home, perhaps a consistent gift each year, such as a book, that you purchase on their behalf. The book can be relevant to the child's interest as they grow. It can be personalised with a note. Make sure that you send a photo of the item and send it to the family member who requested the gift. However, children should also learn that by giving your time and putting in an effort to connect, is a gift in itself.

Friends and family can easily send birthday cards or letters via post. However, in some countries, people may complain about the cost of international postage. If that is going to be an obstacle for not sending anything, provide some money for this specific purpose whenever you visit again. Cards and letters can be put in a scrapbook, and over the years, it will become a treasured keepsake.

Weddings

Don't be surprised that you are not invited or don't receive a formal invitation via mail. There is a perception that international postage is expensive, and they will just assume that you can't attend the wedding. Make the bride or her parents aware of the fact that you want to be included in the whole wedding process, whether you attend or not.

If you definitely can't attend, request a recording of the proceedings and lots of photos. Again, offer to pay for your copy of the wedding recording. Ask if someone is willing to take a Tablet inside and have you watch in real-time.

However, we've found that on the big day, people are so busy and pre-occupied that they don't add photos in real-time on social media. You may only see photos a day or two later, which can be very frustrating and leaves you feeling "forgotten".

Christmas and other holidays

We are using Christmas as an example here because that is what we know, but there are many religious and cultural events that you as a family may want to keep.

For most people, Christmas can be the most depressing time of the year when you are away from family. Invite other "scatterlings from all over the world" to your Christmas celebrations and start a new tradition with an "International Christmas lunch". In Australia, you will quickly have a "new" family for Christmas.

To get into the Christmas spirit, attend "Carols in the Park" (local councils organise this) and other Christmas events organised by churches and religious organisations.

Make Christmas decorations with photos or the names of loved ones on Christmas baubles to decorate your new tree and to remember them during the holidays.

Get the whole family together for a Skype/Zoom session while Grandpa reads the Bible story. This is a great way to get all the family together from all over the world, even when they are scattered around the globe. Time zones are an issue, but where there is a will, there is a way. It is only once a year.

Take an annual family Christmas photo and design a Christmas card for family and friends.

Create a digital Christmas countdown with photos of your life and experiences in Australia and email it to loved ones.

Easter

In some ways, Easter can feel even worse than Christmas. Your work colleagues will chatter about who they are going to visit during Easter, and after Easter, they will tell you in detail how great it was seeing the family again. At least with Christmas, you have New Year celebrations to numb the Christmas blues.

One way to combat this is to take leave and go on a holiday from after Easter to the next Monday. Get out of the house and go camping or see another city. Just get your mind off not being with family. A new family tradition can be hot cross buns for breakfast, nicely toasted with butter and marmalade.

Family gatherings

Make sure to organise a big family gathering or two, to cater to both sides of the family, when you go back to visit. This should be a big bash to create awesome memories. It must make up for the previous gatherings you couldn't attend.

Top tip: *Don't visit each and every family group separately. It is not only exhausting, but you may also eat and drink more than usual! Don't talk only about yourself at these gatherings; often, your family can not relate to your life in Australia. Ask questions about the lives of your loved ones and what the main events/milestones had been so far. Be interested in what is going on in their lives too.*

Send family and friends an annual questionnaire to complete. It is fun and can be informative. It provides you with new insights and topics for future conversations and gift ideas for children's birthdays.

Funerals

Sadly, family and friends die, and this could be a difficult thing to deal with when you are in Australia.

Talk to the family back home via phone, Skype, or email. Share stories and memories of the person who died.

Be part of the decision-making process regarding the funeral arrangements and letter. For example, I wrote a poem for my Dad, and it was printed on the back of his funeral letter.

Request the funeral letter, photos and if possible, a recording of the funeral if the person was close to you.

Request personal belongings you can use as keepsakes.

When you return to your home country, visit the physical burial site, and take more photos.

Have your own private, family ritual of saying good-bye.

If you don't have words to sympathise with, have a look at

this website for ideas: www.acknowledgements.net/words-of-sympathy

Provide each family member space and time to mourn in their own unique way. Don't tell your partner or children that they should stop crying.

If you can't cry, watch a tear-jerker movie such as *Steel Magnolias*, *Dying Young* or *Marley and me*. Just get the emotions out of your system. You must mourn.

Connect with family in your home country after the funeral and share what was shared by others at the funeral.

Create a photobook with all your memories and others' stories. An Australian colleague recorded all the eulogies and stories at his mother's funeral. He then typed it verbatim and collated it in a booklet for all his siblings.

Take time off from work to acknowledge the loss and give yourself time to mourn. If you internalise your grief, you won't open yourself up to receive support. Nobody at the office can read your mind to offer support. They might just experience you as rude or disengaged, and not relate to your added distress of not being at the funeral.

Don't mourn on social media. If it is the anniversary of a birthday or day of passing, do something for yourself, such as going for a massage or take the day off from work and have lunch with a friend (in Australia we call these "mental health days").

Plant a tree in Australia, in memory of the person and always refer to it as: "Grandpa's tree" for example.

MANAGING MIGRATORY GRIEF AND LOSS

Get out and about

Find distractions, like visiting The Immigration Museum in Melbourne, for example. Frequent visits to the museum will remind you of other migrants' journeys to Australia. You will be so grateful for modern transport and communication media after each visit, and you will know that it is a shared journey of many Australians.

Explore your new environment together by getting onto a train and visiting new places in the city or outer suburbs.

Join or start a **"With One Voice"** choir. Singing has proven neuro-scientific benefits to combat loneliness and depression.

No experience needed and you can apply for a $10 000 grant to start a choir in your area:

www.creativityaustralia.org.au

Keepsakes

Keep treasures, a memory box, journal, photo album. Create a Pinterest account and search for creative ideas to keep memories of people and places alive.

Start with a photobook to tell your family's migration story to the next generations in Australia.

New public holidays

Make an effort to make public holidays, like **Australia Day** and Anzac Day, a special occasion. Find creative ideas on www.australiaday.com.au

Organise a "Harmony Day" lunch at the office or in your community. **Harmony Day** is usually celebrated in March to celebrate cultural diversity, with the slogan: Everyone belongs. Register your interest on the website and receive heaps of ideas and decorations: www.harmony.gov.au

Family talks/evenings

Nobody in your home country or here in Australia is going to acknowledge your migratory grief and loss. At least provide opportunities at home for yourself and the family to talk about it and share your feelings and insights with each other.

Have a family movie night with popcorn and other home country nibbles and watch a movie or recorded music event from your home country.

Play board games in your native language.

Organise a family karaoke event with only native country songs and music.

Revisit your family goals and vision board.

Create a "You've got mail"-ritual to encourage children to share their anger, hurt and frustrations, as well as what they are grateful for and praise, where necessary.

ASSISTANCE IN AUSTRALIA

In Australia, help is just a phone call away.

Kids Helpline

Phone and online support for children 5 to 25 years.
Tel: 1800 55 1800
www.kidshelpline.com.au

Lifeline Australia

Tel: 13 11 14
www.lifeline.org.au

Parenting South Australia

For other Parent Easy Guides including: Thinking divorce? Family break-up, After the break-up, Dealing with a crisis, Young people – feelings and depression.
www.parenting.sa.gov.au

Parent Helpline

Tel: 1300 364 100
For advice on child health and parenting.

BeyondBlue

Phone 1300 224 636 – 24 hours
Information, phone, and online support for people suffering grief and loss - www.beyondblue.org.au

Youth BeyondBlue

Information and support for young people dealing with anxiety or depression.
www.youthbeyondblue.org.au

ReachOut
Information, tools, and support for young people dealing with everyday troubles or tough times.
www.au.reachout.com

Kids Matter
Information for parents and carers about children, grief, and trauma – www.beyou.edu.au

Trauma and Grief Network
Information and resources for parents and carers of children and young people affected by trauma, grief, and loss.
www.tgn.anu.edu.au

GriefLink
Information and resources for those experiencing death-related grief.
www.grieflink.org.au

Raising Children Network
Information about raising children
www.raisingchildren.net.au

Most public libraries will have or will be able to get, books about loss and grief for adults and children. Have a talk to the librarian, asking for books suitable for your child's age. Bookshops with specialist sections for children are also likely to have books about loss and grief, suitable for your child's age.

*The information and advice provided in this chapter are not intended to replace advice from a qualified practitioner. Use it as guidelines and to find creative ideas.

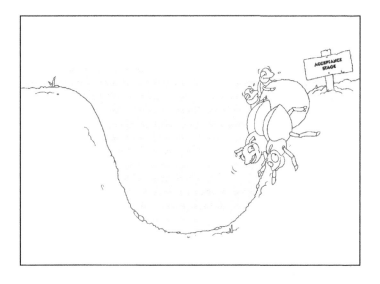

The final stage of culture shock is the Acceptance stage.

14

YOUR RELOCATION BUDGET

"A budget is telling your money where to go instead of wondering where it went."

~ *Dave Ramsey (American businessman and millionaire)*

Being a migrant, you probably know someone who has walked this immigration road to Australia ahead of you. You can learn valuable lessons from them, or maybe you know someone already living in Australia who can show you the ropes.

As we mentioned in the introduction, it is important to remember that every person and family is different. Nobody's circumstances are the same as yours. Your home country friends or family may paint only half the picture, as their children could be older, or they might have a bigger budget.

All the information on Facebook and forums could just be sending you on a wild goose chase. From over a decade's experience in moving migrants and ex-pats to Australia, we have come across many variables and many different situations.

We encourage you to research and to listen and learn from other fellow countrymen, but in the end, you need to do what is right for your family.

Start on the right foot, and you will set yourself up for a positive future in Australia.

Budgeting

These are the first questions we are always asked: "Do I have enough money? How much is enough?" And of course, without fail, we hear the surprised cries at the exchange rate of foreign currency to the Australian dollar.

When it comes to budget, plain and simple, it depends on how comfortable you want to be. For this reason, we can't give you exact numbers, but we can provide you with what needs to be in your budget, and we can share what we have found works well. It is up to you to make the budget bigger or smaller, depending on your standard of living.

There are many ways to save money when relocating, and most of them require that you are savvy about what you do. To be savvy about an international move, you need to have foresight and guidance.

Consider the time of year you are moving. Most migrants will move around the school year cycle. The children will finish school in their home country around December and commence their new school year in Australia in late January.

This is of course high season and the busiest time for removalists – and with more than enough work, they aren't necessarily competitive in price. You will find yourself trying to find accommodation over the festive season, which means double the cost. Airline tickets in high season are much more expensive too.

It is also the quietest time for rental properties in Australia, meaning you could take even longer to find a new home. Think about it, who moves to a new house at Christmas time? The rental market is quiet from early December until the second week of January. Even then, many estate agents are operating with minimal staff because they are only back in full swing after Australia Day on the 26th of January.

If you find yourself moving over the festive season, we would recommend a short "look-and-see" visit, but make sure your timing is perfect (Chapter 3). There are three parts to your move that we will discuss individually to give you the best advice:

Part one: The moving budget.

Part two: The arrival budget.

Part three: The settling-in budget.

The moving budget will touch on your removal costs, accommodation, flights and moving with pets. This is basically the components that make up the physical move of your family and personal belongings.

The arrival budget covers the expected costs for the first four to six weeks. We highlight common mistakes people make and how to avoid them.

The settling-in budget covers all those costs around your new home and school.

PART ONE: THE MOVING BUDGET

Your moving costs and temporary accommodation are the biggest expenses and vital to the success of your move. They are also your biggest stress points if something goes wrong, so careful planning here is imperative.

You don't want to be left high and dry by removals companies. Or, if you have tried to save money on your accommodation, arriving and finding the accommodation is next door to a construction site!

Remember, a positive arrival will set you up for a positive experience in Australia.

Look around your house. Your current home is your comfort zone. That vase you inherited from your Grandmother, your beautiful sofa, the children's favourite toys and even your entertaining platters are all part of your existence. These things are your possessions and worldly goods.

Handing your treasured possessions over to someone to pack in a container, load onto a freight ship on top of hundreds of other containers, to endure all weather conditions across the ocean, is something you should take very seriously!

"Cheap and cheerful" does not always work, but you also don't want to be taken advantage of by removalists. It is a big decision, and the sooner you can make this decision, the better. You can start your removals process about a year in advance. Locking down a quote six months in advance is not that uncommon. Also refer to Chapter 3, which covers much more reading on this topic.

If you are contemplating airfreight, make sure that you have identified what is going by air and what is going by sea. Distinguish items around the home with coloured post-it notes, for example, blue for sea freight, green for airfreight, yellow for fragile items. These items will need to be pointed out to the companies coming to inspect your goods. They will need to consider the volume for sea and air freight, respectively. Fragile items might require special packing or crating, so you should distinguish them too.

If there are items in your home that you are not shipping, then make sure they are either out of the house or put aside, so they are not included in the volume calculations.

Airfreight is a good idea if you have children but otherwise try to avoid it. Airfreight costs are calculated by the weight of your consignment, while sea freight costs are influenced by volume rather than weight. Consider your air freight package carefully – books, for example, are heavy.

There are faster, cheaper ways of sending smaller consignments via air. As a benchmark, for 4-6 standard carton boxes, 40 centimetres (cm) x 40 cm x 60 cm, you will pay around \$3 500 - \$4 500 for air freight with a removalist, depending on the weight of the contents.

You could also consider:

1. **Freight forwarding** – check that they include your customs and quarantine clearance.

2. **Unaccompanied luggage** – you need to drop this at the airport and collect it again. Consider the timing.

3. **Excess baggage on your flight.** You can load additional luggage at the time of buying your aeroplane tickets, or a few days prior to your flight. This comes with a warning, though. Think of your airport transfer or hired vehicle. If you are travelling with small children, they can be enough of a handful going through customs and at the airport.

Other removals components that can influence the cost of your move and should be given due consideration:

1. **Specialised packing:** Crating of artwork, sculptures and figurines, large televisions or even an odd-shaped antique or precious doll's house.

2. **Access to your property:** Do you live on an estate, which the truck cannot access? Perhaps your driveway is a narrow road with overhanging trees. Will a huge truck with a container have access to the house? If there is no clear

access, usually within 20 metres (m) of your door, then additional labour costs and a shuttle vehicle may be required.

3. **A shuttle vehicle** may incur at least three extra packers because one person must stay with the container at all times, another to drive the shuttle vehicle and perhaps a third packer to cover the extra distance and make sure there are enough people to get the job done in time.

4. **Staircases:** Most moving quotes will include the ground and first level, but if you have a flight of stairs from the driveway into the house, and then perhaps a double-storey, that is classified as three flights of stairs. Extra stairs, extra labour.

Also, be aware of the above-mentioned issues for your future home in Australia. You may not know what the house will look like but be aware that additional costs could be charged further down the road.

Only about 20% of families we assisted with their moves incurred these extras costs. In Australia, there are not many homes within estates, but overhanging trees or tri-storey townhouses may be an issue.

Shipping and transport timelines

As mentioned before, the shipping time will influence your costs for accommodation and other arrival expenses. Usually, shipping time will vary, depending on where you are coming from, but it will never be less than five weeks.

A move from a city located inland takes longer because the container has to travel to a harbour city for shipping, whereas a harbour city move will be quicker.

Be aware that the shipping companies will quote you the "time at sea", not the full transport. The time at sea is sort of guaranteed, but they can't control customs, quarantine and vessel loading times.

Insurance

Insurance is a hidden cost on your removal quote, but something to be aware of during your budget process. Work out what you believe the replacement value is of your goods. Knowing this figure ahead of time means it can be added into your quote and budget from the start. This will make various quotes more realistic and comparable.

The insurance is based on a percentage of the value you place on your home contents.

It is unusual for the removal quotes to include your insurance in the total figure because most people have not thought this far yet, and the quotes just have an innocent little percentage sitting there.

When, closer to your move date, you provide a value, suddenly your budget may be blown out. This percentage should be anything between 2.5% and 4% of the value you place on your belongings.

Real-life lesson

With most removals' companies, jewellery is not included in your shipping insurance. Yes, they move it, but in the fine print, there are often exclusions for things like jewellery. Please confirm that these items are covered under your own personal insurance or travel insurance.

Sadly, we spoke to a lady not long ago, who took off her rings to pack boxes and at the end of the day they were gone. She not only had removalists in her home, but also an electrician and people who were buying her furniture. It was not a happy ending when she discovered the rings were gone and no longer insured!

Accommodation

This is second on the budget list and usually your second biggest cost. It is also one of those big decisions you can make early on.

Remember, you need to book a large block of time to stay in one place, so give this your earliest attention. You can usually always tweak the dates slightly once your flights are booked, but you do want to lock down 4-6 weeks of accommodation well in advance. You don't want to pack your bags and move around from one hotel to another. Your accommodation options in Australia:

Hotels:
We don't recommend this only because they have no cooking facilities and it will completely blow your budget if you have to eat out all the time. Hotel rooms can be cramped when you have many suitcases.

Serviced apartments:
In your home country, you might search for "self-catering", but in Australia, they are better known as "serviced apartments". These apartments have cooking facilities, are usually cleaned weekly and have easy access facilities such as a pool or gym.

Further advantages to serviced apartments are:
1. There are additional rooms in the building, so you can usually extend or shorten your stay easily according to your needs at the time. Check the cancellation policy before you book. Most often you will receive a refund if you provide seven days' notice.
2. You can often negotiate the price by reducing the weekly cleans or asking for a discount for booking as a "long stay".
3. Usually, you don't need to pay the full amount at the time of booking. If you confirm this booking early, then you can "pay off" the accommodation costs. Don't be afraid to ask.
4. The overall cost looks a lot higher, but remember you may obtain a refund, if necessary.

Popular serviced apartment providers are:
1. Quest Apartments, (www.questapartments.com.au/home/locations)
2. Punt Hill (www.punthill.com.au)
3. Boutique Stays are pet friendly. (www.boutiquestays.com.au)

Airbnb or holiday rentals:
Airbnb needs no introduction around the world. It is a great option to feel like a local from day one, and accommodation can often include toys for children or just those little extras that make it more comfortable (www.airbnb.com.au). Airbnb provides a homely feel and usually have helpful hosts to point out local amenities and other services.

However, there are some risks, and when you are planning an international move, risks and unwanted surprises should be avoided. Unfortunately, you must pay the full cost at the time of booking. It is a live booking site, with no alternatives and no refund if you find a rental home quickly. If upon arrival, you are faced with a less than advertised property that you have already paid for, it can make for a very uncomfortable extended stay.

Another popular website in Australia for holiday rentals is Stayz (www.stayz.com.au)

Other options:
Cabins at caravan parks are very cost-effective, but they are few and far between. Caravan parks provide a resort-type feel with options for the children to enjoy themselves. The biggest chain of caravan parks in Australia is Big4 Holiday Parks. It is a good option to obtain a budget price:
(www.big4.com.au/caravan-parks)

Motels:
With motels, you often have the owners on-site, managing the motel. Over the years, we have come to know many motel owners who go above and beyond in making a new family feel welcome.

Motel owners will put you in touch with local services and even provide a reference for your rental application. The only downside to motels is that, like hotels, they do not have cooking facilities, and rooms can be small.

PART TWO: THE ARRIVAL BUDGET

The in-transit phase of your relocation is from the time you leave your home where you are currently living, to the time you arrive at a rental property in Australia. The costs we are discussing here are those other than your accommodation, which is a big spend on its own. Here are some of the hidden costs that you may not have thought of to budget for before.

As mentioned before, this part of the budget will depend on your standard of living.

Eating out in some countries is so common that we find families just default to it upon arrival in Australia. They are jet-lagged and tired, and a big breakfast with fresh fruit juice and a couple of coffees seems just perfect.

For four people, this will set you back a whopping $80 - $100. In your jet-lagged state, you don't take too much notice, until day three when you realise that you have wasted $500 in the blink of an eye!

You need to be realistic when working out this budget, and being realistic when you don't live in Australia can be very difficult. However, we can provide you with the following guidelines to assist with the budgeting process:

Transit costs

Besides the flight costs, allow for food and magazines at the airport. If you have a layover of more than three hours, consider booking an airport lounge. You will eat enough in three hours to cover the cost of fast food.

In an airport lounge, you may have a shower and refresh in peace and quiet. Check the airport website for a list of airport lounges. There are many around the globe where you can "buy" 3 hours' entry or a day.

If you have a long layover, then airports like Dubai and Singapore have airport hotel rooms, where you can sleep on a bed, shower and refresh. If you are flying via Singapore, the airport offers a free tourist shuttle bus for all in-transit passengers. You can't exit the bus, but it is nice to do some sightseeing!

Changi Airport (Singapore) has a rooftop sunflower garden, where you can watch the aeroplanes take off. There is also a movie cinema, games rooms, orchid gardens, and many wonderful shops.

This is just an example of what is available. Check the website of the airport you are flying through – you will be amazed by what is on offer.

Airport transfer (car transfer) should be considered for both sides of the world. Families often forget their luggage when booking. Remember, the number of bags will have a direct implication on the cost.

If you have many big suitcases and you are a family, then a maxi van (minibus) may be needed. Don't become a statistic and hire a cheap little hatchback from the airport just to realise your luggage won't fit! This is a mistake people realise a couple of days before leaving or when they arrive in Australia. This could be a breaking point for families who are tired, jet-lagged, emotional and stressed.

You will have to rent a car for at least the first two months, and then you can buy a car when you have your own address. For both your driving licence and registering a car, you have to provide "proof of address" in the form of an electricity bill or a similar document with your name and address in Australia.

Food

Eating out in Australia is expensive. Eating in, while you are in a serviced apartment, can also be tricky, especially if you have chosen something cheap where the frying pan is buckled, and the knives are blunt.

While you are in temporary accommodation, you will spend your days on the road looking for a home, visiting schools, buying a car, and orientating yourself.

It is nice to have lunch at a newly discovered café which offers free WIFI. But a toasted sandwich and drink will set you back around $10-$15 per person. Below are some typical food outlets you can look up online.

Work out an average of what lunch or dinner might look like for your family:

- The Groove Train
- Coffee Club
- Bakers Delight
- Brumby's
- Grill'd

Fast food outlets:

- Domino's Pizza
- Nando's
- MacDonalds ("Maccas", as Australians call it)
- Red Rooster
- KFC
- Hungry Jacks

If you are taking the option of four to five weeks of temporary accommodation, then work out a budget for food during this time.

For the first week at least, you will eat out a lot more. Don't be too conservative in your budget estimate. If you have done your homework and have set yourself a weekly food limit, you will not find yourself quite as stressed in week one! Foresight and good planning will keep you on track and reduce the stress levels.

You can also get online and see what an average grocery shop might look like for your family. This comes with a warning, though! There are cheaper ways of filling the pantry when you arrive, but for the purpose of working out your cost of living, our mainstream grocery stores will give you a good enough average, even slightly inflated.

Take a look at Coles and Woolworths. There are also many local fresh food markets, high street grocers and other options such as ALDI and IGA, but it is a little trickier to check their prices online, and they are not in every state around the country.

PART THREE: THE SETTLING-IN BUDGET

Monthly rent

When your application for a rental home has been accepted, you will need to pay at least one month's rent in advance, plus one month's rent as a deposit. That is the minimum, but for budget purposes, plan to have ten weeks rent ready to go. This must be in your Australian bank account by the time you start looking for a home.

Once accepted on a property, you have to pay the first month's rent within 24 hours, or the property will be given to the next applicant in line.

Research rental prices on the internet using RealEstate (www.realestate.com or Domain (www.domain.com.au). Refer to Chapter 4 to understand the marketing tactics used by the estate agents on the internet.

There are many pitfalls, and a relocation consultant could be very valuable for giving good advice.

Rent is advertised weekly on these sites, but you do pay your rent monthly, in advance and usually on the anniversary of the day you move in. For example, if your lease starts on the 18th, you will pay your rent on the 18th of every month. When the online rental price is $500 per week, you cannot just multiply this by four to get your monthly rent.

The rent is worked out on a formula, so you pay the same amount each month.

There are slight variances, but this is the formula most used: *$500 per week, divided by 7 days, times 365 days, divided by 12 months = your monthly rent*

Utility connections

Gas, water and electricity connections can be arranged within a week. With the help of a relocation consultant, it can be accomplished within about 48 hours. The bills are invoiced monthly or quarterly – you may choose the frequency. Your connection costs are included on your first invoice.

These are minimal:
1. Water: Less than $50
2. Electricity: Less than $80
3. Gas: $80

Internet service can be costly, but the market is getting more and more competitive, so the prices are coming down. However, Australia is still one of the most expensive countries in the world for internet access. The National Broadband Network (NBN) is rolling out across the country, but this is not necessarily any cheaper just yet. You should budget around $120 per month for unlimited service. There are deals from around $89.

You can research the following companies:
- TPG
- Optus
- Vodafone
- Telstra/Big Pond

If you rent, any **council tax and other costs** are the landlord's responsibility and are included in your rent. Depending on where you live, you may need a parking permit if you are parking on the street. This is around $75 per vehicle per year.

If you rent, you are **not required to insure** the house (building), only your personal belongings need insurance.

Rental furniture
You can rent furniture packages in Australia, and they will even work out much cheaper than your short-term accommodation.

This is a cost-effective option if you find a rental property within a couple of weeks of arriving and are still waiting for your own stuff to arrive. Some people choose to camp, but after a week or so, it really loses its appeal!

Furniture rental suppliers charge delivery, installation, and collection costs. There is a tipping point of whether it is still cost-effective when compared to staying in temporary accommodation.

If your sea freight takes eight weeks, then you need to move into your new home around the four to five-week mark. If you only hire furniture for two weeks, plus the installation fees, then it is cheaper to stay in temporary accommodation.

A relocation consultant will have access to corporate rates for furniture hire and will be able to arrange your hire with a reputable supplier. You can also hire baby furniture; this could include car seats, wooden cots, high chairs, and many more.

Cost-saving tips:

1. *If you have family and friends in Australia, you can borrow furniture from them. It is a bit of a pain loading it all, but it will save you money. You then just need to hire your washing machine and other white goods.*

2. *Settled fellow countrymen will be more than happy to assist "newbies" with extra furniture, selected kitchenware and much more.*

3. *You could buy camping furniture, blow-up mattresses, picnic tables and chairs and a few bean bags. In Chapter 6, there are several links and ideas.*

4. *You may even consider house sitting for someone who is going on holiday for three months. You can look after their house rent-free if you feed the pets!*

Schooling costs

There are vast cost differences between state, private and semi-private schools. We explained it in more detail in Chapter 5, but as this is the budget section, it is important to mention the following:

Enrolment fees for the different types of schools are:
State schools are basically FREE to apply and enrol.

Private schools require around $400 for an application fee and sometimes as much as $1000 per child for enrolment. This will be deducted from the child's first term school fees.

Semi-private schools usually require around a $100

application fee, and if there is an enrolment fee, it will be around $500. Most of the time, you are just asked the first term's payment.

School books and stationery:
You will need to buy schoolbooks and stationery. High school students will need a laptop or tablet, although most primary schools require a BYOD (bring your own device), rather than supply shared PC's in a classroom.

School uniforms:
State school uniform costs may vary, but a good budget amount would be around $300 per child, including school shoes. Each child will need a school uniform and PE/Sports kit.

Private and semi-private school uniforms can be very expensive - it could cost $800 - $1000 per child. Many of these schools have a second-hand uniform shop so buy that blazer second-hand.

They literally wear these blazers to and from school, so don't spend $300 on a new blazer! If the child represents the school on any first-team sport level, he or she will need a "first" blazer too.

Private schools require specific sports kit for each sport, and your child will be exposed to a few different sports. They will belong to a School House and need the kit for their house. You also have to buy a uniform for summer and winter respectively.

If you are relocating to Australia for the start of the new school year, be warned that the summer uniforms are worn in Term 4 and Term 1.

If your child commences with a school in January, you will need to purchase the winter uniform by Easter for Term 2.

Cost-saving tips:

1. *Create your new support network of other parents at the school as soon as possible. Very often this network will rally around you with school uniform their children have outgrown. We received almost all the school clothes for the summer uniform (free) and only had to buy a few items for the sports kit.*

2. *Buy one cardigan and note the frequency of it being used. Only if your child wears it regularly, you can buy another one.*

3. *If other people assisted you with handing down school uniforms, please pay it forward and do the same for the next immigrants that are arriving.*

SUMMARY OF RECOMMENDATIONS

Being presented with all these costs can make you feel overwhelmed and your dream out of reach. But trust us. You are better off knowing these things in advance than when you arrive, and you are caught unaware, unprepared and with no options or alternatives.

Not all of these costs mentioned in this chapter will be relevant to your situation. If they are relevant, you will at least be prepared.

We highly recommend engaging a relocation consultant to assist you with your relocation. You might not see the value in the service before you arrive, but a good relocation consultant will:

- Save you from spending too much or unnecessary money.
- Guide you through the process of shortlisting suburbs and renting a property.
- Provide your rental application with the edge against local applicants who have a credit history in Australia.
- Finding a home in 3-5 weeks after arrival will save you the money you would have paid for temporary accommodation.
- Assist you with utility connections.
- Guide you through all the important decisions you need to make quickly.
- Help you prioritise and compare schools that suit your children.
- Be a trusted confidant who is batting on your team!

15

AUSSIE SLANG AND HUMOUR

"I know all those words, but that sentence makes no sense to me."

~ Matt Groening (Cartoonist, writer and animator)

Did you know that there are over 225 languages spoken in homes across Australia? This is mostly thanks to the early settlement of Europeans and our Asian neighbours. After English, the most popular language is Italian, then Greek and Cantonese.

Australia has its own born and bred form of English that can be hard to understand, though.

AUSTRALIAN JOKES
In your home country, you have jokes that no-one else would understand if they are not native to that specific country. Likewise, there are inside jokes in Australia that you may also not understand at first.

A very good example of this is something as innocent as a bird, called the budgie.

Do you know the little bird that comes in blue, green and yellow? They are cute, chirpy things you are likely to see in a cage in your home country. We also have budgies in Australia. In fact, we even have our own "singing budgie", Kylie Minogue.

We also have a "budgie smuggler". This is an item of clothing that was worn by ex-Prime Minister, Tony Abbott, while he was interviewed for TV on the beach one morning. It created a media hype and nationwide laughter. You see, a "budgie smuggler" is the Australian name for a Speedo bathing suit, a rather small piece of clothing mostly worn by lifeguards and elite swimmers. We will leave that to the imagination...

There are a couple of stories in Australian history that sums up the Australian way of life. One of those is the disappearance of Prime Minister Harold Holt in 1967. Don't get me wrong, his apparent drowning off the beach in Portsea, Victoria, was taken very seriously, and his body not being found resulted in years of speculation. What Aussies do find "funny" is that his memory was commemorated with the Harold Holt Swimming Centre - pretty ironic for someone who drowned!

Then they have a saying: "Doing a Bradbury." Steven Bradbury epitomises the Australian culture in never giving up, always giving it a go and being honest. We encourage you to watch the YouTube video of "Last Man Standing" (2 min 20 sec).

In summary, this is his story:
Steven represented Australia in two Winter Olympic Games for short stack ice skating but had never done his best. The first time, he crashed and broke his neck. With the second Winter Olympics, he was impaled on another skater's blade. His third Winter Olympics was held at Salt Lake in 2002. Through perseverance, good skating and a few things that went his way, Bradbury made it to the finals!

In his own words: "The only way I could get anywhere in the final was to get on the ice and stay out the way." It worked. During the last turn of the 90-second race, all five other skiers crashed out. Bradbury was the only one to finish, and he took gold for Australia.

He was as honest an Aussie as you can find, without a big ego, but he was realistic and came out on top. So, when you hear someone is "doing a Bradbury", you know it refers to accidental success.

DIFFERENT WORDS, SAME MEANING/OBJECT

UK	US	AUS
Advertisement	Commercial	Ad
Alcohol	Liquor	Alcohol/liquor
Aubergine	Eggplant	Eggplant
Autumn	Fall/Autumn	Autumn
Baked potato	Jacket potato	Baked potato
Banking card machine	Card machine	Eftpos machine
Biscuits (sweet)	Cookies	Biccies
Biscuits (savoury)	Crackers	Biccies
Block of flats	Apartment building	Apartment/unit
Bottle store	Liquor store	Bottle shop
Carpark	Parking lot	Carpark
Carry bag	Tote/shopping bag	Carry bag/plastic bag
Cheque (account)	Check (account)	Cheque (account)
Chemist	Drugstore/Pharmacy	Chemist/Pharmacy
Chicken	Chicken (coop)	Chook (shed)
Chips	French fries/fries	Hot chips
Clothes pegs	Clothespins	Pegs
Cooler box	Cooler	Esky
Coriander	Cilantro	Coriander
Corn flour	Corn starch	Corn flour
Courgette	Zucchini	Zucchini
Crisps	Potato chips	Chips

UK	US	AUS
Curtains	Drapes	Curtains
Duvet	Comforter	Doona
Eraser (pencil)	Eraser (pencil)	Rubber (pencils)
First floor	Second floor	First floor
Flat	Apartment	Flat
Flip flops	Flip flops	Thongs
Fortnight	Two weeks	Fortnight
Gherkin	Pickle	Gherkin
G-string	Thong	G-string/bum floss
Ground floor	First floor	Ground floor
Holiday	Vacation	Holiday
Jumper/pullover	sweater	Jumper
Knickers	Panties/underwear	Undies
Lawyer	Attorney	Lawyer/solicitor
Lift	Elevator	Lift/elevator
Lipbalm	Chapstick	Lipbalm
Longer Heavier Vehicles/Super Lorries	Trailer truck/big rig	Roadtrain
Lorry	Truck	Truck
Medicine	Drugs	Medicine
Minced beef	Ground beef	Mince
Mobile phone	Cell phone	Mobile
Mosquito	Mosquito	Mozzie
Motorway	Expressway	Freeway
Nappy	Diaper	Nappy
Petrol	Gasoline	Petrol/Fuel
Pharmacy	Drug store	Chemist
Plaster (Elastoplast)	Band-Aid	Bandage/plaster
Post	Mail	Post

UK	US	AUS
Postcode	ZIP code	Postcode
Power plug	Wall plug	Powerpoint
Prestik	Sticky-tack/ Tic 'n' Stik	Blu-Tack
Queue	Line	Queue
Red/green pepper	Bell pepper	Capsicum
Rubbish (bin)	Garbage (trash can)	Rubbish (bin)
Scones	Biscuits	Scones
Sellotape	Scotch tape	Sticky tape
Shop	Store	Shop
Soft drink	Soda	Soft drink
Spring onion/ Shallots	Scallion	Shallots
Sunbathe	Sunbathe	Sunbake
Sweets	Candy	Lollies/sweets
Take-away	Take-out	Take-away
Tap	Faucet	Tap
Tipp-Ex	Wite-Out	White out
Toilet	Restroom	Loo/toilet
Torch	Flashlight	Torch
Tracksuit	Sweatsuit	Trackie dacks
Traffic circle	Traffic circle or rotary	Roundabout
Trainers	Sneakers/runners	Trainers/joggers
Underground	Subway	Metro
Utility vehicle	Pickup	Ute
Weedeater/Trimmer	String trimmer	Whipper snipper
Wellington boots	Rubber boots/ mud boots or goloshes	Gumboots/wellies

AUSTRALIAN ABBREVIATIONS

During your home search, you might see the following abbreviations on the real estate adverts:

BIC or BIR – Built-in cupboards or built-in robes

LUG – Lock up garage

OSP - Off-street parking

A/C – Air conditioning

Split system: This is not central heating; it is a wall-mounted unit that can supply heating and cooling. This should be a red flag to you that there may not be heating or cooling in all areas of the house.

Euro laundry: This is a European style laundry system, where the laundry taps are behind a cupboard in the passage, main bathroom or under a staircase.

OVERHEARD CONVERSATIONS

Weather or traffic reports:

"Ah, it's ordinary out there!" - It's actually horrible or bad.

"It's a real stack!" – A traffic accident (cars stacked) or just congestion.

Grocery shopping:

"Do you have Flybuys?"

"Everyday rewards card?"

"Do you have a community benefits card?"

These are typical questions you may be asked depending on where you are shopping. They are the loyalty cards for that particular store. See more in Chapter 6.

At footy games, a barbie or other social events:

"Arrive before the bounce." – To start a footy match, the umpire will throw the ball down really hard, so it bounces up, and whichever team catches it, has the possession.

You may also hear this phrase in a weather report: "We should see some sunshine in time for the bounce."

"How do you earn a crust?" – How do you earn money? What is your job?

"He's all over that like a seagull with a chip." – Seagulls are known to swarm all around you if you arrive at the beach with your fish and chips, a favourite pastime in summer when the sun sets late.

"Like a rat up a drainpipe." – To do something quickly.

"As useless as a glass door on a dunny/ a pork chop at a synagogue/ or a letterbox on a tombstone." – A useless person.

"Going off like your Nanna in Spotlight." – "Nanna" is a grandmother, and "Spotlight" is a craft shop. This refers to a person getting really excited about maybe a ball of wool, a croquet pattern, fabric or coloured paper.

AUSTRALIAN NAMES
- Byron - Bizza
- Gary - Gazza
- Kieran - Kizza
- Julie – Jules
- Margret, Marilyn – Maz
- Richard - Richo
- Sharon - Shazza
- Sophie – Soph
- Tarryn - Tazz
- Tom/Tim – Tomo/Timbo
- Veronica - Vero

You can also expect that if they can't re-name you, then you could be BIG Pete, Big Bob or just Ol'Mate.

AUSTRALIA'S "UNOFFICIAL" NATIONAL ANTHEM

Waltzing Matilda

Written by Andrew Barton "Banjo" Paterson in 1895

Once a jolly swagman camped by a billabong
Under the shade of a coolibah tree,
And he sang as he watched and waited till his "Billy" boiled,
"You'll come a-waltzing Matilda, with me."

Chorus:
Waltzing Matilda, waltzing Matilda,
You'll come a-waltzing Matilda, with me,
And he sang as he watched and waited till his "Billy" boiled,
"You'll come a-waltzing Matilda, with me."

Down came a jumbuck to drink at that billabong,
Up jumped the swagman and grabbed him with glee,
And he sang as he shoved that jumbuck in his tucker bag,
"You'll come a-waltzing Matilda, with me."

(Chorus)

Up rode the squatter, mounted on his thoroughbred.
Down came the troopers, one, two, and three.
"Whose is that jumbuck you've got in your tucker bag?
You'll come a-waltzing Matilda, with me."

(Chorus)

Up jumped the swagman and sprang into the billabong.
"You'll never catch me alive!" said he
And his ghost may be heard as you pass by that billabong:
"You'll come a-waltzing Matilda, with me."

AUSSIE SLANG

Ack Willy:	Awol or absent without leave
Ankle biter:	A small child or small dog
Apples, she'll be:	It'll be alright
Are you right?:	Often used as sarcasm too if someone bumps into you and doesn't apologise. Can I help you?
Arvo:	Afternoon
Aussie	Australian (pronounced "Ozzie")
Aussie salute:	Brushing away flies with the hand
Australia:	Straya
Avos:	Avocados
Ambo(s):	Paramedic(s)
Back of Bourke:	A very long way away
Bail out:	Depart, usually angrily
Barbie:	Barbecue (noun)
Barrack:	To cheer on (football team etc.)
Bangers and mash:	Sausages and mashed potato
Bastard:	Can be either a term of affection or the opposite!
Battler:	Someone working hard and only just making a living
Beaut, beauty:	Great, fantastic: "you beaut!"
Bickie:	Biscuit, also expensive ("it cost big bickies.")
Bikie:	Motorbike rider
Billy:	Large tin can used to boil water over a campfire for tea
Bities:	Biting insects
Bitzer:	Mongrel dog (bits of this and bits of that)
Bizzo:	Business ("mind your own bizzo!")
Bloke:	Man, guy

Bloody:	Very hard work ("bloody hard yakka")
Bloody oath!:	That's certainly true
Bludger:	Lazy person, layabout, somebody who always relies on other people to do things or lend him things
Blue:	Fight ("he was having a blue with his wife.")
Blue, make a:	Make a mistake
Bluey (or Blue):	Blue cattle dog (named after its subtle markings) which is an excellent working dog. Everyone's favourite all-Aussie dog.
Bob's your uncle:	It will be alright, there you go
Bodgy:	Of inferior quality, same as "dodgy"
Boogie board:	A hybrid, half-sized surfboard
Booze bus:	Police vehicle used for catching drunk drivers
Boozer:	A pub
Bottle-o:	Liquor shop (we also have a drive-thru bottle-o)
Bottle shop:	Liquor shop
Brass razoo:	Very poor ("he's not got a brass razoo.")
Brekkie:	Breakfast
Brickie:	Bricklayer
Brizzie:	Brisbane, the State capital of Queensland
Buckley's chance:	No chance ("New Zealand stands a Buckley's of beating Australia at football.")
Buck's night:	Stag party, male gathering the night before the wedding
Bullshit, to:	To tell lies
Bush:	The hinterland, the outback, anywhere that isn't in town
Bushie:	Someone who lives in the bush
Bushranger:	Highwayman, outlaw
BYO:	Unlicensed restaurant where you have to bring your own grog

Cark it:	To die, cease functioning ("the ol' dog carked it.")
Chewy:	Chewing gum
Chokkie:	Chocolate
Chook:	A chicken
Chrissie:	Christmas
Chippy:	A carpenter
Chuck a sickie:	Take the day off sick from work when you're perfectly healthy
Chuck a yonnie:	Throw a stone
Click:	Kilometre ("it's 10 clicks away.")
Cop that!:	Take that!
Coldie:	A beer
Come a gutser:	Make a bad mistake, have an accident
Compo:	Workers' compensation pay
Cozzie:	Bathers (swimming costume)
Cranky:	In a bad mood, angry
Cream (verb):	Defeat by a large margin ("they creamed the opposition.")
Crook:	Sick, or badly made
Cut lunch:	Sandwiches
Cut snake:	Very angry ("he is as mad as a cut snake.")
Dag:	A funny person, nerd, goof, also fashion sense ("his daggy clothes …")
Daks:	Trousers
Damper:	Bread made from flour and water
Deadset:	True, the absolute truth
Dero:	Tramp, hobo, homeless person (from "derelict")
Dinkum	True, real, genuine ("I'm a dinkum Aussie"; "is he fair dinkum?")
Dinky-di:	The real thing, genuine
Dipstick:	A loser, idiot ("He's a complete dipstick!")
Dob (somebody) in:	To split somebody

Dobber:	A tell-tale ("Kate dobbed me in to the teacher.")
Doc:	Doctor
Docket:	A bill, receipt
Doco:	Documentary
Dog:	Unattractive woman
Down under:	Australia and New Zealand
Drink with the flies:	To drink alone
Druggie:	Drug addict
Dummy, spit the:	Getting very upset at something
Dunny:	Outside lavatory or toilet
Durry:	Cigarette
Earbashing:	Nagging, non-stop chatter
Esky:	Cooler box, large insulated food/drink container for picnics, barbecues etc.
Fair dinkum:	True, genuine
Fair go:	A chance (to give a bloke a fair go)
Flake:	Shark's flesh (sold in fish & chips shops)
Footy:	Australian rules football
Fruit loop:	Fool
Firies:	Fire brigade
Full:	Drunk
Galah:	Fool (Named after the bird of the same name which flies south in winter – to a colder climate!)
Garbo:	Municipal garbage collector
G'Day, Gidday:	Hello
Give it a burl:	Try it, have a go
Good oil:	Useful information, a good idea, the truth
Good on you:	Good for you, well done
Greenie:	Environmentalist

Grog:	Liquor, beer ("Bring your own grog, you bludger!")
Grouse (adj.):	Great, terrific, very good
Gyno:	Gynaecologist
Heaps:	A lot ("Thanks heaps!", "They earned heaps of money.")
Hoon:	Hooligan, mostly used for people who perform burnouts on the street or drive badly (dob them in on the hoon hotline!)
Hottie:	Hot-water bottle
Icy pole:	Popsicle, lollypop, frozen
Jackaroo:	A male station hand (a "station" is a big farm/grazing property)
Jillaroo:	A female station hand
Joey:	Baby kangaroo
Journo:	Journalist
Jumbuck:	Sheep
Kindie:	Kindergarten
Knock:	To criticise
Knock back:	Refusal (noun)
	Refuse (transitive verb)
Larrikin:	A bloke who is always enjoying himself, harmless prankster
Lippy:	Lipstick
Liquid laugh:	Vomit
Lob, lob in:	Drop in to see someone ("The rellies have lobbed.")
Lollies:	Sweets, candy
London to a brick:	Absolute certainty ("It's London to a brick that taxes won't go down.")
Loo:	Toilet
Lurk:	Illegal or underhanded racket

Mate:	Buddy, friend
Macca's:	Mcdonald's, also known as "the golden arches"
Macca's run:	Mcdonald's drive through or a late night ice cream treat
Middy:	285 ml beer glass in New South Wales
Milk bar:	Corner shop that also sells take-away food
Milko:	Milkman
Mob:	Group of people, not necessarily troublesome
A group of kangaroos
Mongrel:	Despicable person
Mozzie:	Mosquito
Mug:	Friendly insult, gullible person ("Have a go, yer mug!")
Never Never:	Outback, the centre of Australia
Ninkum poop:	A fool
Nipper:	Young surf lifesaver
No-hoper:	Somebody who'll never do well
Not the full quid:	Not bright intellectually
Nuddy:	Naked
Offsider:	An assistant, helper
Oldies:	Parents ("I'll have to ask my oldies.")
Outback:	Interior of Australia
Oz:	Australia!
Pash:	Passion, infatuation, kissing passionately
Pav:	Pavlova – a rich, creamy (Australian) dessert
Pill:	A person's head
Plonk:	Cheap wine
Polly:	Politician

Pom, pommy:	An Englishman (derived from "pomegranate", as they are seen to have rosy cheeks!)
Postie:	Postman, mailman
Pot:	285 ml beer glass
Povo:	A poor person, from the word poverty
Pozzy:	Position (Get a good pozzy at the football stadium)
Prezzy:	Present, gift
Quack, or off to the quack:	The doctor, or off to the doctor
Quid, make a:	Money, earn a living ("Are you making a quid?")
Quid, not the full:	Low IQ
Rage:	Party
Rage on:	To continue partying ("We raged on until 3am.")
Rapt:	Pleased, delighted
Rats:	Don't care ("I couldn't give a rats!")
Raw prawn:	Bullshit, to be generally disagreeable
Razzo:	Not worth much, another phrase is "brass razoo"
Reckon:	You bet/absolutely
Rego:	Vehicle registration
Rellie:	Family relative
Right:	Okay ("she'll be right, mate!")
Ripper:	Great, fantastic
Road train:	Big truck with many trailers
Roo:	Kangaroo
Rotten:	Drunk ("I went out last night and got rotten.")
Rubbish:	To criticise
RDO:	Registered day off

Salvos, the:	The Salvation Army
Salute, Aussie:	Brushing flies away
Sanger:	A sandwich
Schooner:	A large beer glass in Queensland, Small beer glass in South Australia
Scratchy:	Instant lottery ticket that you scratch to win
Screamer:	Party lover
Screamer, two pot:	Somebody who gets drunk on very little alcohol
Screamer, take a:	In footy - take an awesome mark/catch
Servo:	Petrol station
Shark biscuit:	Somebody new to surfing
Sheila:	A woman
She'll be right:	It'll turn out okay (Aussie mantra!)
Shoot through:	To leave or pass by quickly
Shout:	Turn to buy – usually a round of drinks ("It's your shout.")
Shonky:	Unreliable or untrustworthy
Sickie:	Day off sick from work (to "chuck a sickie" means to take the day off sick from work when you're perfectly healthy!)
Skite:	Boast, brag
Smoko:	Smoke or coffee break
Snag:	A sausage in bread
Spagbol:	Spaghetti Bolognese – at least once a week!
Sparkie:	Electrician
Spit the dummy:	Get very upset at something
Sprung:	Caught doing something wrong
Station:	A big farm/grazing property
Stick it in your kick:	Stick it in your pocket
Stickybeak:	Nosy person
Stone the crows:	Heaven forbid!
Stuffed, I'll be:	Expression of surprise

Stuffed, I feel:	I'm tired
Strewth:	Exclamation, mild oath ("Strewth, that Chris is a bonzer bloke!")
Stubby:	A beer bottle
Stubby holder:	Polystyrene insulated holder for a stubby
Sunnies:	Sunglasses
Surfies:	People who go surfing, usually more often than they go to work!
Swag:	Items/luggage - carried by a swagman.
Swagman:	Tramp, hobo
Tall poppies:	Successful people
Ta muchly:	Thank you very much
Technicolour yawn:	Vomit
Tee-up:	To set up an appointment
Tele:	Television
Thingo:	Wadjamacallit, thingummy, whatsit (anything you can't remember)
Thongs:	Cheap rubber backless sandals
Throne, on the throne:	Toilet, on the toilet
Thunderbox:	Toilet
Tipple:	Wine (usually) with dinner
Tinny:	Can of beer, or also a small aluminium boat
Togs:	Swimsuit
Too right!:	Definitely!
Top end:	Far north of Australia
Truckie:	Truck driver
True blue:	Patriotic
Tucker:	Food
Tucker-bag:	Food bag
U-ie:	U-turn, to "chuck a U-ie" is to make a U-turn

Uni:	University
Unit:	Flat, apartment
Up oneself:	Have a high opinion of oneself ("He's really up himself.")
Ute:	Utility vehicle
Veg out:	Relax in front of the television (like a vegetable)
Vegies:	Vegetables
Vego:	Vegetarian
Vee dub:	Volkswagen (VW)
Waggin' school:	Playing truant
Walkabout, it's gone:	It's lost, can't be found
Whacko:	An exclamation ("You beauty!")
Whinge:	Complain
White pointers on the beach:	Topless (female) sunbathers
Wobbly:	Excitable behaviour ("I complained about the food and the waiter threw a wobbly.")
Wog:	The British called any non-British living in the UK a "wog". "Wogs" in Australia typically refer to Europeans.
Wombat:	Somebody who eats roots and leaves (Vegetarian)
Wowser:	Straight-laced person, prude, puritan, spoilsport
Woop-Woop:	Mythical village in the outback, beyond the black stump in Never Never
Wuss:	Wimp or nervous person
XXXX (pronounced "four X"):	Brand of beer made in Queensland
Yabber:	Talk (a lot)

Yakka:	Work (noun)
Yanks:	Americans
Youse:	You
Zees:	Referring to ZZZ's in getting some sleep

16

IMPORTANT DOCUMENTATION

"I have so much paperwork.
I'm afraid my paperwork has paperwork."

~ D Gabrielle Zevin (American author and screenwriter)

Paperwork before, during and after your move will seem endless. There are many documents that go with your visa application, moving quotes, customs forms and medical forms.

Then you move, and there is more paperwork for your rental application, driver's licence, tax number, insurance, utilities, and the list goes on!

What documents can you prepare before you leave your home country?

REFERENCES FOR A RENTAL PROPERTY
Identify people in your work and social circle who would be willing to provide you with **written reference letters**. Once you have left your home country, those people might not have

any interest in helping you, but while they see you on a daily basis, they are far more obliging.

When you are presenting your rental application to a real estate agent, remember that they have quite a few applications for each property to submit for the landlord's approval. They are not going to phone your home country references when another applicant has his "mate" down the road in the correct time zone. Written references make the estate agent's life easy, and when his or her life is easy, yours can be easy too.

Most migrants we relocate have been home-owners for years already, and the thought of renting a property is daunting and quite a change to their mindset.

The chances are that you are selling your home or renting it through a **real estate agent**. Contact them and ask if they are prepared to write a **professional reference** about you and your home. Words that would impress an Aussie landlord, or any landlord for that matter, are: "house proud", "easy to work with", "prompt payments", "efficient".

Your accountant, lawyer and pastor or anybody else in a position of authority, can write a **character reference**. Two character references are ideal. More than that would most likely be a waste of time.

A **rental application** will need to be completed for each person living in the house over the age of 18 years, so consider this when you are obtaining references.

If you are moving with a pet, you are required to state this on your rental application. We highly recommend that you prepare a **pet application**, with a small photo and a brief description of your pet. Include the microchip number and anything that makes it seem more official and professional.

MEDICAL RECORDS

You will need to take all your **medical records** with you, so speak to your general practitioner (GP), dentist, paediatrician and other applicable specialists in advance to find out how this can be done. Some have a hard copy of the records, and others have it electronically.

In any event, your medical practitioners will need some time to prepare the documents for you, so don't leave this to the last minute. Remember, these documents have to be in English.

The same should be said for **prescription medicine**. There is a list of prescribed drugs you may not bring into Australia. Review this and speak to your doctor to try and obtain a supply to get you through the first three months in Australia. You are legally only allowed to bring in three months' supply of prescribed drugs.

Your pharmacist should be able to supply you with the components so you can find similar medication in Australia. We have found that Australian GP's and pharmacists are able to check most foreign medicine online and prescribe similar equivalents: www.tga.gov.au/entering-australia

SCHOOL
The school will require these documents as a minimum, so please do not put them in your sea freight; otherwise, you will not be able to complete the enrolment process:
1. Children's birth certificates.
2. Passports.
3. Visa status.
4. Previous school reports.
5. If you are arriving midyear, then bring the school reports for the current year and the end of year report for the previous year.

IMMUNISATION REPORTS
Make sure that these reports have been updated according to Australian requirements. For further information, please visit this site: www.health.gov.au/health-topics/immunisation

Depending on your state, there are a couple of ways to get immunisations up to date and in a format that schools in Australia will understand. Your local GP in Australia can do this, but it can take some time to have the national register updated.

The quickest way is to check your local council website and see when the child and healthcare clinic is open in your area. These nurses are usually the same nurses who carry out immunisations at local schools. They understand the system backwards and can have you up to date in no time. They could also provide an action plan to catch up with immunisations if needs be.

TAX FILE NUMBER

You will need a tax file number before you start work. You can apply online, but only once you have arrived in Australia.

Make sure you are on the Australian Tax Office (ATO) website to apply. Some sites charge you, and this is completely unnecessary:

www.ato.gov.au/Individuals/Tax-file-number/Apply-for-a-TFN/

MEDICARE

Medicare is the Australian government's medical care and provides healthcare to citizens, permanent residents and those who are temporary residents from countries with a reciprocal health care agreement. If you are eligible for Medicare, then you should apply right away. Refer to Chapter 6 for more detailed information.

Medicare gives you immediate access to public health care in Australia, support with the cost of out of hospital care and subsidised medicines. Medicare does not cover adult dentistry, optical or ambulance services.

You will need to visit a Medicare office in person. Every member of the family must attend. There is no formal appointment; you arrive at the offices, take a number from the machine and wait for your turn.

You should do this soon after arriving if you are eligible. You don't need a permanent address for your Medicare cards to be posted. You can provide a friend's or work address. You can later update your details online.

To apply for Medicare, you will need:
1. Passport.
2. Visa.
3. The application form and any other recommended paperwork can be found on this website:
   www.servicesaustralia.gov.au/individuals/subjects/how-enrol-and-get-started-medicare

DRIVER'S LICENCE

You will need to have proof of address to apply for your driver's licence, so leave this until after arriving in Australia.

You will need:
1. Passport.
2. Your home country's driver's licence.
3. Any information relating to restrictions on your licence, like optical glasses.
4. Proof of address (a utility bill with your name and home address on it or your rental lease).
5. Payment will depend on how long you purchase a licence for: three, five or ten years.

You will need to make an appointment at the authority in your state (refer to the websites provided in Chapter 6).

When you arrive, take a seat and wait to be called. You will produce your paperwork for checking, and the assistant will take your photo and ask you to perform an eyesight test.

The whole process takes around 30 minutes, and your licence will be posted to your home address within a couple of weeks.

The recommended sequence of events after your arrival:
1. Buy a public transport card.
2. Obtain a mobile phone with a "Pay-as-you-Go"- option.
3. Apply for Medicare, if you are eligible.
4. Apply for a tax file number.
5. Get immunisation records.

6. Find a school, if you are sending your children to a state school.
7. Find a house, if you are not regulated by school zones.
8. Connect the utilities when you have secured a rental property.
9. Obtain a phone contract to replace the Pay-as-you-Go.
10. Obtain your driver's licence.
11. Buy and register a car.
12. Complete your insurance requirements.

PERSONS AUTHORISED TO CERTIFY IDENTIFICATION DOCUMENTATION

Copies of all documents must be legible, and photographs must be in colour and clearly identifiable. Certification must be on the front of the photocopied document, not the reverse unless it would render the photocopy illegible.

The person certifying the document must note that it is a true copy of the original document, which he or she has seen, and print his or her name, the date and qualification that enables them to certify the document and sign the declaration.

Below is a list of persons who are authorised to certify photocopies of identification documents:

- Chiropractor
- Dentist
- Legal practitioner
- Medical practitioner
- Nurse
- Patent attorney
- Pharmacist
- Veterinary surgeon
- Police officer
- Registrar, or deputy registrar, of a court
- Sheriff
- Sheriff's officer
- Teacher employed on a full-time basis at a school or tertiary education institution.

You will need Justice of the Peace if you are renewing your home country passport or applying for Australian PR or citizenship.

Most police stations will offer a Justice of the Peace service, but some restrict it to only certain days so they can manage their workflow.

While on the subject of passports, you will require ink fingerprints. This is not available in police stations anymore; they all use electronic scanners. You will need to contact your State Police headquarters and make an appointment for a set of ink fingerprints. These must be on the correct paperwork supplied by the consulate.

APPS TO DOWNLOAD BEFORE YOU LEAVE

Mobile phones and specific apps can make life easier. You are probably drowning in all the paperwork by now. These can help with your planning, budgeting and research.

Moving Checklist Pro

The Moving Checklist Pro app comes with pre-loaded notes, to-do lists and a planner. This is a must! You can customise it according to your needs, and it has over two hundred household items loaded so that you can organize and arrange them effortlessly, and know in which box to find what. Anything you need to remember, such as school deadlines, can be put into the app – categorise and date it and you are sorted. It not only covers what you need to do for your move but also school follow-ups, job interviews and heaps more.

RealEstate and Domain

These apps are for house hunting in Australia. You can view homes on the map, as a list or by open inspections. You can also set up alerts and notifications of homes coming onto the market that meets your criteria of price, suburbs and needs.

Taxis and UBER

There are apps for Uber and taxis in all cities and towns.

Navigation and live traffic

The Waze **app** lets you check traffic routes to estimate what your commute might look like even before you. People often underestimate the size of Australia and think things are not far away. We would also recommend **Google maps**. Not only can you see traffic, but you can also monitor fire alerts in your area or suburb.

Public transport

There are various apps for each mode of transport in each major city. Check which is relevant to your area, for example, in Sydney it is **Opal Travel**, in Melbourne, the **PTV** app covers all modes of transport, but you might also want **tramTRACKER**.

You can use these apps to plan a route between landmarks, addresses and stations. It will show you which mode of transport to use (train, tram or walking), stops where you need to change lines, the commute times and even if there are walking distances between the transport services.

Your airline

Download the app for the airline you are using. You can save your booking in the app and will receive alerts if your flight is delayed or if there are any changes.

You might also want to check SeatGuru to check where is best to sit in a particular aircraft, to get the most legroom, get your meal first or maybe check if there are USB ports and charging points at your seat. Skyscanner is good to check prices. Many Australians use Webjet for domestic flights.

Trip Advisor and UrbanSpoon

These apps are useful to find restaurants and see local reviews.

Communication and social media

You probably have **Facebook, LinkedIn** and **WhatsApp** already on your phone. Facebook Messenger is used more frequently in Australia, but WhatsApp is also growing in popularity. If you don't want to miss out on invites to events and communication at schools, it would be a good idea to create a Facebook profile and get your head around its inner workings. You don't have to post anything, and you can set the privacy settings so that you feel comfortable with them. Of course, don't forget **Skype**!

Top tips:

1. *If your parents and family are not computer savvy, please make sure to teach them how to use Skype, for example. Older parents sometimes forget, and we would recommend writing the steps down (and if possible, add screenshots to illustrate the steps).*

   There is nothing more frustrating than when you are sitting in front of your computer in Australia, ready to chat with Grandparents back home who just can't manage to get Skype going. If you/they download any new software onto their computers, make sure that they write the passwords down. They do not remember them!

2. *Update your music playlist or make an "aeroplane playlist", and maybe even add some guided meditation, podcasts or audiobooks.*

APPS TO DOWNLOAD IN AUSTRALIA

Once you have arrived, you should also add:

Weatherzone

Includes a radar image and can send you alerts of thunderstorms or danger warnings in your area. Some weather apps also provide alerts for pollen counts and UV-rates for the day.

Grocery shopping

Woolworths Shopping Online and **Coles Online** Home Shopping, allow you to scan items in your pantry and add them to your list. You can save earlier lists, and just repeat them for the next shopping trip. If you are going into the store to pick your own items, the app will sort your shopping by aisle so you can find things faster.

We would also recommend **Catch of the Day** for bulk buying of anything from cleaning products to breakfast bars! It is all online, and deliveries are quick.

Classified and second-hand goods
Gumtree and **Ebay** for classified ads, as well as auction items.

Gumtree also has a jobs app – but this is mostly for handyman jobs. These jobs are now mostly moving over to **Airtasker**.

Gumtree and **Facebook Marketplace** for buying and selling second-hand furniture and goods.

The **Freecycle Network®** is made up of 5,000+ groups with over 9 million members across the globe. It's a grassroots and entirely non-profit movement of people who are giving (and getting) stuff for free in their own towns and keeping good stuff out of landfills. Membership is free, and everything posted must be free, legal and appropriate for all ages.

Used cars
Carsales app, mostly for used cars.

Jobs
Load the **SEEK** or **JORA** app if you are job hunting and set up notifications and alerts.

Menulog or UberEATS
For take away food deliveries. We all deserve a night off sometimes!

FURTHER READING AND RESOURCES

Chapter 1:
Anon. (2018). Dung beetle. [online] Available at:
https://en.wikipedia.org/wiki/Dung_beetle

Byrne, M. (2012). The dance of the dung beetle [video recording, TED Talk;
online] Available at:
https://www.ted.com/talks/marcus_byrne_the_dance_of_the_dung_beetle?
language=en

Hadley, D. (2018). 10 fascinating facts about dung beetles. [online] Available
at: https://www.thoughtco.com/fascinating-facts-about-dung-beetles-
1968119

Information about Maslow's hierarchy is readily available on the internet.

Slade, E. & Manning, P. (2018). Why isn't the world covered in poop? [video
recording, TED-Ed; online] Available at:
https://www.youtube.com/watch?v=uSTNyHkde08

Chapter 2:
Anon. (2000). Australian History. [online] Available at:
https://www.australianexplorer.com/australian_history.htm

Anon. (2018). Ausflag: Our own flag. [online] Available at:
http://www.ausflag.com.au/

Anon. (2018). Australia's History. [online] Available at:
https://www.australia.com/en/facts-and-planning/history.html

Anon. (2018). Emu. [online] Available at: ttps://en.wikipedia.org/wiki/Emu

Anon. (2018). States and Territories of Australia. [online] Available at:
https://simple.wikipedia.org/wiki/States_and_territories_of_Australia

Department of Home Affairs. (2018). https://www.homeaffairs.gov.au/

Department of Immigration and Citizenship. (2009). Australian Citizenship:
Our Common Bond. [online] Available at:
https://immi.homeaffairs.gov.au/citizenship/test-and-interview/our-
common-bond

Jones, B. (2010). Map of Australia. [image; online] Available at:
www.mapsfordesign.com.

Smith, T. (2018). Red Kangeroo: 11 Facts about Australia's National Animal.
[online] Available at:
https://theculturetrip.com/pacific/australia/articles/red-kangaroo-11-facts-
about-australias-national-animal/
[Note: this image was edited with regards to size, amount of information and spelling].

Chapter 5:
Pollock, D.C. & Van Reken, R.E. 2004. Third culture kids: The experience of growing up among worlds. Nicholas Brealey Publishing, Boston. pp. 185-215.

Chapter 6:
Anon. (2018). A-Z Item List. [online] Available at: http://www.whichbin.com.au/az-items/

Anon. (2018). Australian national sport team nicknames. [online] Available at: https://en.wikipedia.org/wiki/Australian_national_sports_team_nicknames [Note: this information was significantly reduced and shortened].

Anon. (2018). Australian Football League. [online] Available at: https://en.wikipedia.org/wiki/Australian_Football_League

Australian Bureau of Statistics. (2018). Media Release: Census reveals Australia's religious diversity on World Religion Day. [online] Available at: http://www.abs.gov.au/AUSSTATS/abs@.nsf/mediareleasesbyReleaseDate /8497F7A8E7DB5BEFCA25821800203DA4?OpenDocument

Department of Home Affairs. (2018). 100 points identification guidelines. [online] Available at: https://www.homeaffairs.gov.au/ Licensing/Documents/100-points-identification-guidelines.pdf

Chapter 7:
Anon. (2000). Convict Creations. [online] Available at: http://www.convictcreations.com/culture/socialrules.htm#top

Anon. (2017). Australia Guide: Culture, Customs and Etiquette. [online] Available at: https://www.commisceo-global.com/resources/country-guides/australia-guide

Anon. (2018). Australian Customs and Etiquettes. [online] Available at: http://www.indiaeducation.net/studyabroad/australia/manners-in-australia.aspx

Anon. (2018). Australian Culture. [online] Available at: https://culturalatlas.sbs.com.au/australian-culture/australian-culture-etiquette

Belinda. A guide to Australian Etiquette. [online] Available at: http://insiderguides.com.au/australian-etiquette/

Kimmorley, S. (2016). 20 Things about Australian working culture that can surprise foreigners. [online] Available at: https://www.businessinsider.com.au/20-things-about-australian-working-culture-that-can-surprise-foreigners-2015-3

Chapter 8:

Amy in Oz. (2014). No. 18: Tall Poppy Syndrome. [online blog] Available at: https://thingsaussieslike.wordpress.com/2014/11/12/no-18-tall-poppy-syndrome/

Anon. (2000). Convict Creations: Flogging the tall-poppy syndrome. [online] Available at: http://www.convictcreations.com/culture/poppy.htm

Anon. (2014). Top 5 ways to survive culture shock and homesickness. [image of culture shock stages; online blog] Available at: https://ourparticularheart.wordpress.com/2014/06/19/top-5-ways-to-survive-culture-shock-and-homesickness/

Anon. (2018). Acculturation. [online] Available at: https://en.wikipedia.org/wiki/Acculturation

Anon. (2018). Culture Shock. [online] Available at: https://en.wikipedia.org/wiki/Culture_shock

Anon. (2018). Four stages of competence. [online] Available at: https://en.wikipedia.org/wiki/ Four_stages_of_competence

Cutting, R. (2018). 5 Things I've learnt after 5 years in Australia. [online blog] Available at: https://proudlysouthafricaninperth.com/life-in-perth/5-things-ive-learnt-after-5-years-in-australia/

Howell, W.S. (1986). The emphatic communicator. Wadsworth Publishing Company, Belmont.

Kokcharov, I. (2017). Competence Hierarchy adapted from Noel Burch. [online] Available at: https://commons.wikimedia.org/wiki/File:Competence_Hierarchy_adapted_from_Noel_Burch_by_Igor_Kokcharov.svg

McCarthy, P. (2016). Cultural chemistry: Simple strategies for bridging cultural gaps. Cultural Chemistry, Australia. p. 32.

Oberg, K. (1960). Cultural shock: Adjustment to new cultural environments. Practical Anthropology, 7(4):177-182.

Pederson, P. (1995). The five stages of culture shock: Critical incidents around the world. Greenwood Press, London. pp. 1-13.

Townsend, S. (2016). Is tall poppy syndrome embedded in our DNA? [online] Available at: https://www.dailytelegraph.com.au/rendezview/is-tall-poppy-syndrome-embedded-in-our-dna/news-story/e461e79c8b2c22e5de95a25c1551f3ca

Winkelman, M. (1994). Cultural Shock and Adaptation. Journal of Counselling & Development, 73(2):121–126.

Chapter 10:
Cherry, J. (2015). 9 things I learnt about South Africa, thanks to Australia. [online blog] Available at:
https://www.cherryflava.com/economics/business/9-things-i-learnt-about-south-africa-thanks-to-australia/

Chapter 11:
A "faux pas" is the French expression for an embarrassing or tactless act or remark in a social situation, a social blunder. [online] Available at:
https://www.merriam-webster.com/dictionary/faux%20pas

Barkhuizen, GP & Knoch, U. 2005. Missing Afrikaans: "Linguistic Longing" among Afrikaans-Speaking Immigrants in New Zealand. Journal of Multilingual and Multicultural Development, 26(3):216-232.

Bhattacharjee, Y. (2012). Why Bilinguals are Smarter. [online] Available at:
https://www.nytimes.com/2012/03/18/opinion/sunday/the-benefits-of-bilingualism.html

Chan, C. (2016). Why some Chinese Speakers also use Western names. [online] Available at: https://p.dw.com/p/1Ha9r

Department of Social Services. [online] Available at:
http://raisingchildren.net.au/articles/bilingualism_benefits_challenges.html/context/1218

Gollan, T.H. et al. (2011). Degree of Bilingualism predicts age of diagnosis of Alzheimer's Disease in Low-Education but not in Highly-Educated Hispanics. [online] Available at:
www.ncbi.nlm.nih.gov/pmc/articles/PMC3223277

Grosjean, F. (2011). Change of language, Change of personality? Understanding the between language and personality in bilinguals. [online] Available at: https://www.psychologytoday.com/au/blog/life-bilingual/201111/change-language-change-personality

Heald, M. (2017). What is the NATO Phonetic Alphabet? [image of NATO Phonetic Alphabet; online blog] Available at:
https://www.sporcle.com/blog/2017/12/what-is-the-nato-phonetic-alphabet/

Murphy, L. (2008). Accent Deafness. [online] Available at:
https://separatedbyacommonlanguage.blogspot.com/2008/06/accent-deafness.html

Nacamulli, M. (2013). Bilingualism: Learning and speaking two languages. [online] Available at: www.smart-words.org/bilingualism.html
Nacamulli, M. (2013). The benefits of a bilingual brain. [video recording, TED-Ed; online] Available at:
https://www.youtube.com/watch?time_continue=113&v=MMmOLN5zBLY

Satakovski, N. (2013). Unspeakable Acts. The Big Issue, 21 March 2013 Edition: 11

Chapter 12:
Various inputs received from migrants at the Bloom Seminars Migration Research Evening held on 18 August 2018, through emails, social media messages and discussions with specific individuals.

Ashfield, J. (2009). Taking care of yourself and your family: A resource book for good mental health (10th Edition). Peacock Publication, Norwood. pp. 1-39.

Birnberg, C. (2016). 10 Ways to practice self-care with kids. [online blog] Available at: https://carlabirnberg.com/2016/05/09/10-ways-to-practice-self-care-with-kids/

Clark, P. (2017). Practising Self-Care. [online blog] Available at: https://patticlark.org/2017/08/31/practicing-self-care/

Holmes, T.H & Rahe, R.H. (1967). The Social Readjustment Rating Scale. Journal of Psychosomatic Research, 11(2):213-218.

Markway, B. (2014). Seven types of self-care activities for coping with stress. [online] Available at: https://www.psychologytoday.com/intl/blog/shyness-is-nice/201403/seven-types-self-care-activities-coping-stress.

Winkelman, M. (1994). Cultural Shock and Adaptation. Journal of Counselling & Development, 73(2):121–126.

Chapter 13:
Various inputs received from migrants at the Pillars of Power Migration Research Evening held on 18 August 2018, through emails, social media messages and discussions with specific individuals.

Most information used in this chapter was found on the Beyondblue website, www.beyoundblue.org, unless otherwise referenced.

Anon. (2018). Culture Shock. [online] Available at: https://en.wikipedia.org/wiki/Culture_Shock

Ashfield, J. (2009). Taking care of yourself and your family: A resource book for good mental health (10th Edition). Peacock Publication, Norwood. pp. 1-39.

Athan, L. (2009). Children, Immigration and Loss. [online blog] Available at: http://www.griefspeaks.com/id71.html

Cohn, M. (2010). Immigration Losses. [online blog] Available at: http://www.lossesintranslation.com/types-of-losses.php

Parkes, C.M. (1965). Bereavement and mental illness (Part 2): A classification of bereavement reactions. British Journal of Medical Psychology, 38:13–26.
Picard, I.T. (2016). Migratory Grief. The Psychologist, 29:886-893.

Chapter 15:
Anon. (2019). Waltzing Mathilda. [online blog] Available at: https://en.wikipedia.org/wiki/Waltzing_Matilda

Battersby, V. (2007). Australian Language and Culture (3rd Edition). Lonely Planet Publications, Footscray.

Jones, A. (2017). A beginner's guide to Australian slang. [online blog] Available at: https://nomadsworld.com/aussie-slang/

Chapter 16:
Australian Qualifications Framework Council. (2012). Recognition of Prior Learning: An Explanation. [online] Available at: https://www.aqf.edu.au/sites/aqf/files/rpl-explanation.pdf

Skills Certified Australia. What is RPL? [online] Available at: https://www.skillscertified.com.au/rpl

Your Vip Chat Room Code:
YMGVIPCR